College Unzipped

★ AN ALL-ACCESS, BACKSTAGE PASS INTO COLLEGE LIFE,
FROM ALL-NIGHTERS AND EXAM NAIL BITERS,
TO TUITION FEES AND GETTING YOUR DEGREE ★

KAPLAN

PUBLISHING

New York

This publication is designed to provide accurate and authoritative information in regard to the subject matter covered. It is sold with the understanding that the publisher is not engaged in rendering legal, accounting, or other professional service. If legal advice or other expert assistance is required, the services of a competent professional should be sought.

Editorial Director: Jennifer Farthing
Editor: Cynthia Ierardo
Production Editor: Dominique Polfliet
Cover Designer: Carly Schnur

Published by Kaplan Publishing, a division of Kaplan, Inc.
888 Seventh Ave.
New York, NY 10106

Printed in the United States of America

May 2007
07   08   09   10   9   8   7   6   5   4   3   2   1

ISBN 13: 978-1-4195-9635-3
ISBN 10: 1-4195-9635-7

Kaplan Publishing books are available at special quantity discounts to use for sales promotions, employee premiums, or educational purposes. Please email our Special Sales Department to order or for more information at kaplanpublishing@kaplan.com, or write to Kaplan Publishing, 888 7th Avenue, 22nd Floor, New York, NY 10106.

★ TABLE OF CONTENTS ★

★ INTRODUCTION ★

Congratulations—you've been accepted to college, you've graduated from high school, and you're ready to leave home and begin life as a college freshman. I'm sure you've spent countless hours imagining what college will be like—daydreaming about the nonstop social life and newfound freedom you will have. Perhaps, though, you've thought about other aspects of beginning your college career—leaving behind your high school friends, moving away from the safety and comfort of your family, and facing new and unexpected academic challenges. If your mind is racing with all the possibilities that your new life might hold, consider yourself completely normal. ★

Remember, you are not the first and only teenager to go off to college. There have been millions before you, and of course, your very own freshman class is full of them too! That's where this book comes in handy. *College Unzipped* is just what it says—an all-access, backstage pass into college life, from all-nighters and exam nail biters, to tuition fees and getting your degree. But it's more than that too. Want to know the best way to choose a roommate you actually like? Check out Chapter 2. Need the low-down on the Greek system and find out if it's right for you? Turn to Chapter 7. And when it comes to living off-campus, do you know how to go about it? If not, Chapter 8 has your answer! Every chapter in this book offers stories and advice on these one-of-a-kind college experiences.

So what makes me the expert? Simply, I've been there, done that, and loved (almost) every minute of it. That's true for all the contributors to this book. We have all been that nervous high school graduate facing at least four years of uncertainty. We've all lived on mac 'n cheese and ramen noodles. We've studied all night even when there were parties to attend. We've pledged sororities, joined ski clubs, written for the school paper, had nightmare roommates, and survived to tell the tale. So yes, we do know what we are talking about.

But you don't have to take our word for it. Thankfully, everyone's college experience is unique—just as yours will be to you. So, as you are reading this book, don't expect everything to happen exactly as it's written here. Take our advice when it applies to your situation, but don't forget that the college experience is all your own! Enjoy it, because—trust us—this is a once-in-a-lifetime opportunity.

—Sandy Gade
Contributing author

Welcome to the Real World ... Sort of

Y ou may think that leaving for college means that you are now a fully independent adult. Wrong! But that's not necessarily a bad thing. Remember, a little guidance along the way could actually be very helpful as you embark on your new life. In this chapter, we'll lay out the many differences between high school and college. You'll also read thoughts from current and former college students on important topics like embracing your freedom, getting through your course work, and adjusting to your new role as a college freshman. ★

★ HIGH SCHOOL VS. COLLEGE—THE WHOLE TRUTH ★

Clearly, college is a whole different ballgame from high school. Although you might think you know how your life will change, here are some of the ways—for better or for worse— that college is completely different from your high school experience.

The Rules

High school is filled with them. From what classes you take to what time your day begins and ends—decisions are made for you. You spend the majority of your day attending classes, and you are told exactly what you need to do to graduate.

In college, rules become guidelines. No one tells you which classes you need to take or how to plan your schedule so that you take all the classes required for your major, minor, or graduation. You have much more free time during the day, and you are expected to manage your own time between studying and extracurricular activities. If there are rules (for example, no lying, no cheating, no stealing, and no underage drinking), you are expected to follow them. Remember, high school may have been mandatory, but you are at college by choice. If you break the rules you may face expulsion; there's no law stating that you have to receive a college education!

Academics

High school classes tend to have fewer students, and reading assignments are usually reviewed during class time. Teachers take attendance, reinforce assignments and deadlines, give tests more often, and give you a grade for everything from homework assignments to pop quizzes.

College courses may have as many as 150 students, and you should not expect your professors to review in class everything you are assigned to read for coursework. Many professors do not take attendance, and your final grade may be based solely on a midterm and final exam.

Social Life

In high school, you may have had a curfew. Your social life may have revolved around extracurricular activities or hanging out at the mall with your friends. Whether you realize it or not, there is a structure to your social life in high school.

In college, you are on your own. No one is there to tell you when to go to bed, when to study, or how much time you can spend just hanging out with your friends or chatting online. If you are the type of person who needs structure, you might find it difficult to self-regulate your schedule.

★ WHICH IS BETTER? ★

These comparisons between high school and college are not to say that one is better than the other. On the contrary, it's just to highlight some of the important differences between what you already know and what you will face. Here are ten thoughts from college students on their impressions of the differences between high school and college.

" If you flew through your classes in high school . . .
brace yourself. College is a whole new world! "
—**Biology/Chemistry Major, Denison University**

" You can cram and slide your way through high
school, but it is difficult to do that—and do well—
in college. Force yourself to be disciplined and diligent.
It will pay off. "
—**English/French Major, Cornell University**

" High school is nothing like college. You actually have
to make an effort in college. "
—**Biology Major, Clemson University**

" You will spend a lot more time doing homework in
college. Many teachers believe that their class is your
only class. "
—**Psychology/Biology Major, Saint Louis University**

" High school teachers teach you everything you need
to know. College professors assume you're going to
teach yourself. "
—**Chemical Engineering Major, University of Virginia**

" For the first time in your life it's YOUR responsibility to make sure your work gets done. Mom and Dad aren't there to watch over your shoulder. If you don't do your work, you'll fail—so do it for yourself. Anyway, it feels better doing it for yourself than for your parents. "
—**Biometry and Statistics Major, Cornell University**

" What most people don't realize is that you don't learn from the books you are reading, you learn from the application of that knowledge. High school tests often quiz memorization skills. That's a handy talent to have, but unless you can apply what you are learning, the whole process is a waste. "
—**Political Science Major, St. Joseph's University**

" A lot of people get through high school without doing much work. If you've taken AP courses or some accelerated courses, be glad you did, because those help. There is a lot more independent work involved with college. If you can study independently and learn from a book, you will have a great advantage. "
—**Math Major, Carleton College**

" College is not more difficult than high school, except that now you are battling a thousand distractions. "
—**Psychology Major, New York University**

" If you were truly doing what you were supposed to do in high school, college academics aren't that different. Just remember that there usually isn't a homework score to bring your average up, but every class is designed so that you can bomb one test and still get an A. "
     —Political Science Major, Colorado State University

★ INDEPENDENCE DAY ★

So it's your first day on campus—you are free at last . . . now what? Here are ten thoughts from those who've been there.

" Freedom is like a gallon of ice cream—you can overdo it and eat the entire thing at once, but you'll be pretty sick of it afterward. "
     —Political Science/Chinese Language Major, University of California—Irvine

" It was great to get away from home. The sense of freedom and doing whatever you want helps you mature faster, I think, because your parents aren't there to push you. You just have to do what you feel is the right thing to do. "
     —Pre-Law/Mass Communications Major, Ohio State University

" Exercise your newfound freedom moderately. Don't overdo it because your opportunity to attend college can easily be taken away if you fail academically. "
—**Chinese Language Major, University of California—Irvine**

" The college experience helps merge young adults into the real world. During my freshman year in college I was faced with paying numerous bills, balancing my checkbook, doing my own laundry, and cooking and cleaning. "
—**Psychology/Criminology Major, Florida State University**

" I actually matured faster. Once I had the freedom I had been longing for, I found out that there really was not much that I wanted to do that I had not been able to do before. "
—**Economics Major, University of Alabama—Tuscaloosa**

" I could do what I wanted when I wanted. It didn't matter if I felt like going to get a Slurpee from 7-Eleven at 3:00 AM. I didn't have to ask permission. It was great! "
—**Biology Major, Mary Washington College**

" I did everything my parents told me not to do, made up my own mind about what I thought was right and wrong, and eventually came to the same conclusions as my parents. Funny, isn't it? "
—Biology Major, College of Charleston

" At first I definitely went a little crazy, but after a while I realized what I needed to do and I did it. Unfortunately, my freshman grades are what will probably keep me out of a great graduate school. "
—Accounting Major, Utah State University

" A little craziness never hurt anybody—unless you go downright wild. Have fun, do things you've never done before, go to parties (you don't have to drink), go on dates. I personally loved "going out." You can't stay up till 2:00 AM forever, so enjoy it while it lasts! "
—Mass Communications Major, Northeastern State

" Freedom is great until you need your family. I took off, went out all the time, never called home. But when you get sick, stressed out, or nervous and you need a comforting word, it's nice to have that connection. "
—Neuroscience Major, University of Rochester

CAMPUS ORIENTATION—A CRASH COURSE

Although you do have a lot of independence when you first arrive at college, you are definitely provided with guidance through this transition. Although many students choose to exercise their independence by ditching the voluntary freshman orientation, this could be a mistake. After all, these programs are designed to teach you about everything that is available to you on campus. Here are ten thoughts about first impressions of moving to campus and freshman orientation.

> " I thought I was the only one who was nervous, but as it turns out, everyone felt exactly the same way I did! "
> —**Biology Major, Boston College**

> " I assumed that everyone was much more confident than I was, but eventually I realized that all students struggle in some way—I wasn't alone. "
> —**English Major, Princeton University**

> " At first I felt lost at my huge university, but it turned out to be a smaller community than I expected. "
> —**English Major, Rutgers University**

" At orientation everything is thrown at you at once and it feels very overwhelming, but you are not asked to know everything right away. Just know that they are exposing you to as many things as possible to get you excited about the school. "

—**Biology Major, University of Central Florida**

" It's a real paradox, the orientation experience, because although it was miserable and seemed point-less, it definitely made a lasting impact—and being in a new place where I didn't know a single person, those ridiculous "getting-to-know-you games" helped me make some connections with people. I needed to know that I wasn't alone. "

—**Art and Design Major, LaGrange College**

" I noticed that people of the same background tended to stick together. Unfortunately, this was the way it was throughout college. I wish people had branched out more. "

—**Pharmacology Major, University of Connecticut**

" It seemed like everyone was really nice. Slowly, I found out who really was a nice person . . . and who wasn't. Be careful who you trust at first! "

—**Psychology Major, Muhlenberg College**

" Don't forget to bring those touches from home—
photos of friends and family definitely help when you
are feeling homesick! "

    —Photography Major, Rochester Institute of Technology

" My roommate laughed at me when I woke up the first
day at 8:00 AM to go to the library orientation. I had the
last laugh when she needed to research a paper for
her class. "

    —Italian Studies Major, Emory University

" I thought professors were these scary, unapproachable
people. Turns out most professors are happy to help
students achieve their best. "

    —Physical Therapy Major, Ithaca College

★ TIPS FOR ADJUSTING TO COLLEGE ★

The excitement of going away to college can quickly become
overshadowed by reality during your first semester at school.
You may have imagined an endless parade of fraternity and
sorority parties and bonding with your roommate only to find
yourself alone on a Friday night while your roommate is

down the hall with his/her significant other. The best thing to do is to embrace the fact that you may need more time to adjust to your new life than you thought. You should know that with the many good times that school has to offer, there's also times when you are going to be stressed out, homesick, and ready to return to "old" life in high school. As long as you are aware of this, you will be able to weather the bad times and continue to look forward to good times as well.

Of course, there are some students who hit the ground running and from Day One are having the time of their lives. That's great, although more rare than you might imagine. One of the best tips for adjusting to your new life is to find a balance. College isn't a nonstop party, nor is it simply an academic endeavor. Do your best to balance your schedule and do everything (studying, partying, whatever) in moderation. You're not just there to learn but to experience.

Finally, knowing what to expect—the good, the bad, and the ugly—is a great way to keep an open mind about the realities of college and to make sure your expectations meet the realities of college life. Keep reading to learn about another major component of your experience as a college student—life in the dorms!

★ T W O ★

Life in the Dorms

C hances are, as a freshman, you are going to be required to live on campus. That fact means that along with wondering about classes, schedules, and other college unknowns, you will spend some time thinking (and worrying) about one of the biggest unknowns—your roommate.

Whether you're a first-day freshman or a fourth-year senior, how you interact with your roommate will affect your college experience as much as all the late nights in the computer center, the romantic hookups, and the new friends you'll make combined! In the year ahead, you will be sharing private moments, pre-exam stress, and just about everything else with this person—whether you want to or not. ★

Rest assured everyone has roommate issues—from borrowing clothes to borrowing boyfriends, from late-night parties to late-night snoring. But have no fear. Living with another person is an incredible opportunity to learn—both about other people and about yourself. This chapter is packed with quotes and advice from college students and recent grads who have been through it all—and want to make the experience easier for you.

★ CHOOSE YOUR ROOMMATE WISELY ★

At some schools, you have the opportunity to choose your roommate, although at most schools, you are assigned a roommate. The first step to being assigned a roommate is generally a roommate questionnaire. Most college or university housing departments give incoming freshmen these questionnaires to match up compatible roommates. Some schools ask a few general questions about your living and studying habits; others probe deeper with a multitude of questions, right down to your choice of breakfast cereal. Whatever the case, this is not the time to show off your creative writing skills. Here is a list of helpful hints to follow when filling out these forms:

★ **Admit your faults.** If you are messy, admit it. If you like to wake up at 3:00 in the afternoon on weekends, admit it. No matter what you desire to be, your true self will soon be apparent to your new roomie. Don't think that a roommate who is clean will get you to be a cleaner person, because all it will get you is a roommate who is resentful of your messy ways.

★ **Be honest with yourself.** College is a wonderful opportunity to meet students from completely different backgrounds. But while an obsessive-compulsive neat freak and a slob who never changes his sheets can easily get along as friends, they might not make the best roommates. You have to consider how willing you are to live with lifestyles that are so different from yours.

★ **Consider all your options.** To meet the housing needs of their students better, colleges have increased the use of theme housing. No, this does not mean the same as theme parties—no togas here. Theme housing is for like-minded students who want to share similar living situations. A theme could be as general as an all-female dorm. However, common theme living includes "healthy living"—dorms in which alcohol, tobacco, and other controlled substances are strictly forbidden—or "green living"—dorms where ecology, conservation, and environmentalism are a part of everyday life. There are even "academic" housing options at many schools. These dorms have around-the-clock quiet hours so there are a lot fewer distractions to take you away from your studies. Find out what kind of housing options your school has and really consider what you think will be best for you.

★ **Fill out the form.** So this is probably painfully obvious. However, if you don't take the time to fill out the form completely and on time, you're going to be paired up with a random student who also didn't take the time to answer a few questions. Be proactive. If the school is bothering to ask your opinion, take the time to tell them how you really feel.

FINDING YOUR ROOMMATE ONLINE

This isn't the same as MySpace, Friendster, or even Craigslist—there are sites hosted by college housing departments that contain profiles and even photos of potential roommates. You can contact students you think would be a good match, and, if you get along, that request can be passed along to the school. The downside is that reading a profile is not the same as living with someone. Don't let your expectations get too high just by seeing a nice picture or reading a creative profile.

STRANGERS VS. FRIENDS AS ROOMMATES

If you have the opportunity to live with a friend from home, don't think that you're all set for the year. Or if you think living with a stranger spells doom, you should reconsider. Here are ten thoughts from students about their experience with roommates who were strangers or friends before they started living together.

" I'm from a big city on the East Coast, and when I found out my roommate was from a rural town in a state halfway across the country, I wondered why I even took the time to fill out the questionnaire in the first place— clearly they hadn't done a good job! But even though our backgrounds were different, our living styles were perfectly compatible, and I kept the same roommate for four years! "
—Arts Administration Major, Wagner College

" I had talked to my roommate on the phone before we met at college. She told me what she had written on her housing form. It turns out her answers weren't very honest. I spent the entire year feeling lied to. "
—Marketing Communications Major, Emerson College

" You have nothing to lose by rooming with a stranger and only an awesome experience to gain. "
—Political Science Major, Texas Tech University—Lubbock

" I think going into a living situation with two people in a small room was better because of the fact that neither of us knew each other prior to move-in day. We were more respectful than we might have been had we been friends before. "
—Sociology Major, Pennsylvania State University

" Despite the fact that my roommate and I had very little in common when we first met, we got along and remained friends throughout college. I'm glad I was thrown together with her, because otherwise I'm sure we would have never met by ourselves on campus. "
—**Criminal Justice Major, George Washington University**

" I wish I had roomed with someone I did not know. I roomed with my best friend, and we were on each other's back the entire year. It almost ruined our friendship. "
—**Criminology Major, Marquette University**

" My freshman roommate was my best friend from home. DO NOT DO IT. Even though I already knew her, my impression of her changed when I lived with her. She was much less considerate and much sloppier than I had realized. Living with someone is very different from just being friends. "
—**Law Major, Albany Law School**

" It's easy to live with someone who is your good friend— all is fair game, anything can be said, and not as many compromises are necessary because you already have a bond based on more than just sharing a room. "
—**Computer Science Major, Tufts University**

" Don't listen to people who tell you not to room with a friend. My freshman roommate was a stranger and we didn't get along. After that, I lived with friends, and it was a great experience. "

—**Business Major, University of Texas—Austin**

" Forget the myth that living with your best friend will ruin your friendship. If your personalities are compatible, you will be fine. "

—**Psychology Major, University of Missouri**

★ COMMUNICATION IS KEY ★

Imagine this: It's the first day of college and you are surrounded by your parents, a mountain of suitcases, and a whiny little brother. This is not how you want to meet your roommate for the first time!

Luckily, most colleges will reveal the name, address, e-mail address, and phone number of your future roommate a month or two before you move in. All college students offer the same advice: get in touch before move-in day. Why? Because it gives you a chance to uncover what the person you'll be living with for the next year is really like. It will also help you find some common ground so that your first face-to-face meeting will be less stressful.

Read the following ten thoughts about talking to your roommate before move-in day.

" I wished I had talked to my roommate beforehand. We both entered the situation assuming we had the same expectations of each other—but we definitely didn't! Just one little conversation would have helped a lot. "
—**American Studies Major, University of Texas—Austin**

" We talked for weeks before school started, so I already felt like we were friends before we even got there. "
—**Political Science Major, Westmont College**

" Talk about guidelines early on. It only gets harder later. "
—**Food Science Major, University of Florida—Gainesville**

" It helped my roommate and me to ask a lot of 'getting to know you' questions that had nothing to do with our living arrangements. This helped to ease the awkwardness of the move-in because we had an increased comfort level. We also swapped pictures, so when we finally met, it felt like we knew each other a little bit. "
—**English Literature Major, Colorado College**

" We discussed the issues that were important to us on the phone. We developed a mutual respect and trust for each other by doing this. "
—Communication Studies Major, Florida State University

" I wish we had discussed what types of kitchenware we would be bringing. This may seem like a small item, but you try eating cereal with a fork! "
—Philosophy Major, University of Georgia

" We didn't discuss what to bring—and ended up with two TVs, two bath mats, two sets of dishes . . . basically two of everything! "
—International Business and Marketing Major, George Washington University

" We should have talked about not only what we were bringing, but how much. It would have been easier not having so much stuff cluttering up our room. "
—Spanish/History Major, Willamette University

" First impressions are just that—impressions, not how a person really is. You need to take time to sit and talk with a new roommate and find out about her likes and dislikes and past history to really know who she is. "
—Biology Major, University of South Florida

" I wish we had discussed our preferences ahead of time. My roommate got to school first and left me the lower bunk bed because she thought I'd prefer it, although in reality she really wanted to sleep there. I would have rather had the top bunk but didn't say anything because I thought she wanted it! "
—Performance Studies Major, Northwestern University

DORM ESSENTIALS

Aside from the obvious (bed linens, towels, computer), here are some items that you might not think to pack but that most students recommend you bring with you to college:

- ★ Flip flops (for wearing in the shower)
- ★ Batteries
- ★ Flashlight
- ★ Stamps
- ★ Mini sewing kit
- ★ Mini tool kit
- ★ Room or fabric deodorizer
- ★ Umbrella
- ★ First aid kit
- ★ Cold medicine

★ THEY AREN'T ALL HORROR STORIES ★

Due to circumstances beyond my control, I had not one but two different (and equally terrible) roommates my freshman year. But hopefully, this is more often the exception than the rule. If you're lucky, you will have someone who isn't just a roommate but a friend. Here are ten thoughts from students who had a great experience.

" All roommates are weird. The key is realizing that your roommate is weird (and so are you) and deciding to get along with her anyway. When my roommate and I came to this conclusion, the entire year was smooth sailing. "
    —Biology Major, Seattle Pacific University

" I think I was a great roommate. I learned to be extra tolerant and to remember that the other person is going through some of the same things that I was. "
    —Education Major, University of California—Santa Cruz

" On my birthday, my roommate went out of her way to get some balloons to decorate the room. It showed me how thoughtful she was and how lucky I was to have her as a roommate. "
    —Neuroscience and Behavior Major, Wesleyan University

" My roommates were wonderful, but there were still some minor confrontations. We found the only way to solve them was by learning to say what needs to be said in a constructive way. "
—**Philosophy Major, State University of New York—Albany**

" My freshman roommate and I made a deal never to hold a grudge. Little arguments can quickly become catastrophes when confined to closed spaces, so we learned to forgive and forget quickly. "
—**Biochemistry Major, University of California—Davis**

" My roommate was there for advice without judgment when it was desperately needed. "
—**English Major, Villanova University**

" My roommate gave me the confidence to try things at college I had never done before. It was great to know that he was a great friend who was always watching my back. "
—**Engineering Major, Rensselaer Polytechnic Institute**

" My roommate brought me out of my shell so much. She made a huge impact on my life and has changed the way I think about so many things. I was lucky to have been assigned to her. "
—**Psychology Major, Barnard College**

" My roommates were always there to support me.
It meant a lot that I could always turn to them. "
    —**Theater Major, Drew University**

" There were four of us in a tiny, two-bedroom dorm.
I was lucky to have roommates who went out of their
way to keep the place clean and uncluttered. "
    —**Italian Studies Major, New York University**

★ GETTING SET UP ★

The first potential problem you could have with your
roommate is deciding who gets what furniture in the room
and where the furniture should go. When you first set foot
in your dorm room, you'll find yourself in one of three
situations:

Situation 1. You're the first one there. Time to grab
all the best stuff, right? Rein it in a second, partner.
You want to be fair to your roommate. And that
means:

★ *Wait until your roommate arrives.* We know
    you want to get unpacked and start enjoying
    college life, but stop and think about the
    situation from your new roomie's point of

view. What if you arrived second and were left with only one drawer and the worst bed? Do unto your roommate as you would want done unto you.

★ *Make a plan.* Survey the room. Decide what you think is the best way to divide everything evenly. This way when your roommate arrives, you can present her with a clear plan that she can then react to. If your roommate isn't scheduled to arrive until the next day, make sure you discuss the issue in advance.

Situation 2. Your roommate is already there and is in the middle of taking the bigger closet and the nicer desk for herself. Before you start screaming, do the following:

★ *Take a deep breath.* Count to 10 or 20 or whatever number it takes to calm down and assess the situation.

★ *Talk to your roommate.* Tell her (calmly!) that you see she has claimed the biggest closet, so you feel it is only fair that you get the nicer desk.

Situation 3. Your roomie is all set up, has taken everything you wanted, and is probably catching the welcome lunch in the dining hall. Instead of seething over this for the rest of the year or tossing his clothes into the hall, why not try the following instead?

★ *Sit tight until he returns.* Calmly point out that while you appreciate how organized and industrious he has been in setting up the room, he left you no choices.

★ *Meet halfway.* Make some compromises. Say that since he has already unpacked his clothes into the nicer dresser, you would like to switch beds with him. Or if it is the closet that is really important to you, offer to help him move his clothes into the other closet.

★ *Assert yourself.* You have every right to be part of the decision-making process in your own room. If your roommate won't budge, insisting that it's first-come first-served, control your temper and take a nice stroll down to your Resident Assistant's room. (Hey, you had to meet him sooner or later!) One of the RA's jobs is to help resolve roommate conflicts—this qualifies.

DORM ROOM DECOR

Home, sweet home! A shoebox-sized room with drab, cinder block walls, a closet with no door, and metal bunk beds— sounds cozy, doesn't it?

Even the most interior decorating–challenged students would never leave the room this way. In this age of home improvement TV shows, every student has a shot of converting a barracks-like dorm room into a warm, inviting place that doesn't seem divided down the middle but, instead, seems like one room. Here are some simple steps to get you and your roomie started on your dorm room decor:

★ String holiday lights all the way around the room— no matter what time of year, they always bring cheer. Avoid candles—they are usually not allowed in dorm rooms and for good reason—there are almost 25,000 fires each year attributed to unattended candles.

★ Buy several matching bulletin boards or ribbon boards, and each of you cover them with photos of your family, pets, and hometown friends. Or try hanging a tapestry with colors or a pattern that you both like.

★ Plan to buy a rug for your room that matches both your comforters. Carpets reduce noise and give the room warmth. Avoid white or light-colored rugs, so you won't be blamed for the muddy boot prints.

★ RULES OF THE ROOM ★

Learning how to share your space with another person is the biggest roommate lesson you will learn. In a sense, you need to rewire your thinking so you can start considering someone else before you act. (For example, pumping up the volume of your music at 3:00 AM while your roommate is sound asleep before an early-morning exam is not going to make for an easy living situation.) The key is to think beyond yourself.

To get started, here are four areas where you should establish "house rules" before you run into any serious problems.

Quiet Hours for Sleep and Study

Ahhh, sleep. You've been hard at work all day, studying for your biology midterm. You shut off the lights, lie down, and close your eyes, slowly drifting into dreamland. Then—BLAM! The door bangs open and bright light fills the room. You hear your roommate click on his computer and the tap, tap of his keyboard. Goodbye restful sleep . . . hello, roommate confrontation.

Nothing is more precious to a college student than sleep. We all wish for more of it, and nothing makes us more cranky than someone messing with our shuteye schedule. But unfortunately, very few roommates have the same class, exam, and social agenda. Here are some ways to steer clear of the problem:

★ **Find something to mask the noise.** A good option is one of those white noise machines. Drown out your roommate with the soothing sounds of a tropical rain forest or the rhythmic waves of the ocean. Another option is a pair of earplugs, which you can find in any drugstore. Pop 'em in, and silence is yours.

★ **Find something to deflect the light.** Use an eye mask—when your roommate comes home late at night and flicks on the switch, you won't even realize a light is on.

And if you are the one coming home late?

★ **Keep movement to a minimum.** If you know you're going to be out late and will be coming home to a sleeping roomie, plan ahead. Clear the clutter off the floor before you go out so you can make it to your bed without tripping. Place your pj's on your bed for easier access. Take off your clunky heels or heavy boots before you enter your room so you're not clumping around.

★ **Use consideration.** If you are always loud when you come home, don't expect your roommate to go out of the way to stay quiet while you are trying to sleep.

Studying is another reason for having guidelines in your shared space. Very few people have the same study habits. Since this is what you are paying big bucks to do, it is wise to establish the study rules up front. If your roommate can write a paper on Shakespeare while blasting heavy metal music, it doesn't mean you can. Figure out what works for both of you, whether it means studying in the library or having set "study hours" in your room.

Noise Problems and Solutions

The best advice you can get is from someone who has survived a noisy roommate. Here are ten thoughts from students who have been in this position.

" Note to roommate: It is NOT okay to hit snooze 20 times in a row starting at 6:00 AM! "
—**Journalism Major, Syracuse University**

" My roommate was on the swim team and had to be in bed at nine so he could wake up for practice at 4:30 AM! I joined a fraternity and was consequently often out late. We agreed that if I was quiet when I came back at night, he'd be quiet when he woke up in the morning. "
—**Industrial and Labor Relations Major, Cornell University**

" When one of us wanted to go to bed early, we would turn off the ceiling light, but each of us had a small desk lamp that we would use while the other was sleeping. "
—**Criminal Justice Major, State University of New York—Albany**

" If I was watching TV, I had earphones that I could plug into the bottom of the TV if my roommate wanted to sleep."
—**Criminal Justice Major, George Washington University**

" My roommate and I decided early on that if one person had to stay up late and study and the other wanted to sleep, the person who wanted to study went to the study room downstairs in our dorm."
—**Business Administration Major, Boston University**

" My roommate and I made a point of understanding each other's schedules so that we knew not to have any guests over the night before one of us had a big test."
—**International Studies Major, Texas A&M University**

" We set an hour when it was time to stop studying in the room."
—**English Major, University of Oregon**

" If one of us was studying in the room, the other was always respectful—no TV, no loud music, and no endless phone calls."
—**English/Theater Major, Drew University**

" Use a fan with a towel over it to block out late-night noise when you want to sleep. "
   —English Literature Major, University of California—
   Los Angeles

" My roommate and I had opposite going-to-bed/waking-up schedules. We solved this by buying a blue light bulb and putting it in our smallest lamp. This gave enough light to see by so someone didn't trip in the dark, but it wasn't bright enough to wake the person who was sleeping. "
   —Art Major, Skidmore College

Communication

Whether you are a hundred miles from home or going to college in your hometown, the telephone provides the most intimate connection to the family and friends you've left behind. It also holds the promise of Saturday night plans with that special someone, possible information about changes in a study group locale, or a request for a summer job interview. For college students everywhere, the phone is near and dear to their hearts. Fortunately, cell phones (if you have one) mean you've got a direct connection. However, believe it or not, many students still rely on the telephone service provided in the dorms. If this is your situation, establish these rules right away:

★ When you take a message for your roommate, always write it down. There are too many plans for parties and multiple-choice test answers clogging up your brain to have any hope of remembering it.

★ Leave the message somewhere where your roommate is sure to see it. It's a good idea to get a message board of some kind so messages can be seen as soon as someone enters the room.

★ Consider every message important. Even if your roommate's ex-boyfriend has called ten times already, give your roommate every message. It is not for you to determine the merit of the message.

★ Only write the facts. If your roommate's friend calls and says she has to cancel their plans (again) for that night, your message should not read, "[friend's name here] apologizes for being a bad friend. She's canceling again but didn't mention how she was going to make it up to you." You only have to say that "[Friend's name here] had to cancel plans tonight."

★ Discuss beforehand how much information you and your roommate want you to give out to callers about whereabouts and time of return. If your

parents call at 11:00 at night on a Tuesday and you
are at a party but don't want them to know it,
let your roommate know not to say anything.

★ Don't get angry and refuse to take messages.
Instead, talk to your roommate about it.

Sharing Food

You're back from class, but your roommate's still out.
You open the minifridge and spot a slice of chocolate cake.
You know you didn't buy it, but it looks so good. You break
off a piece—just for a taste. Then another piece. Soon, there
are only crumbs left—oops!

You dash off for your next class. Five minutes later, your
roommate comes back to the room. She has been dreaming
of her chocolate cake all afternoon—she even bought a
carton of milk to go with it. She opens the fridge and stares
in horror at the crumbs. Let us tell you—small countries
have gone to war for acts less egregious than this. You are
in big trouble, my friend!

Sharing food without asking is a very sensitive topic.
Students are highly proprietary over their ramen noodles,
instant mac 'n cheese, ice cream, and whatever other small
treats they can afford to cram into their fridge. To avoid
an all-out food fight with your roommate, here are some tips
to keep the grumbling inside your stomach.

At the beginning of the school year, discuss what foods will be shared and what is off-limits. (Financially speaking, it's a good idea to share condiments and staples.)

★ Give each roommate one shelf in the refrigerator for food that is solely his. Have one shelf for common food.

★ Be courteous—never eat someone's last slice of bread or the leftover slice of pizza she's been saving.

★ Do not let your friend or significant other eat the common food or your roommate's food. It's like a restaurant—if you don't pay, you don't eat.

★ Don't blame missing food on Cookie Monster. If you ate it, own up.

★ If you decide to share food, go shopping together and buy foods you both like. If one roommate goes out and purchases all the staples and condiments for the month, remember to reimburse your roommate for half (or whatever your agreed-upon share is).

★ Try to keep it all in perspective. If your roommate ate a handful of potato chips, do not flip out. In the greater scheme of things, greasy slabs of starch are not important enough to fight over.

SAFETY

Personal safety and the safety of your belongings is something all college students must consider. Would your parents invite strangers off the street to hang out in your bedroom? Definitely not. So why is your dorm room or apartment any different?

To ensure your safety, consider the following:

★ Assess the situation. Talk to your roommate about what makes you feel safe in your room. Make sure all the entryways to your room or apartment close properly and are not accessible from the outside if you don't want them to be.

★ Lock the door. It is a good idea to lock the door if you are the last person to leave the room—even if you'll be back shortly.

★ Entertaining strangers. How do you feel about guests? What are your rules about letting people you don't know into your room or apartment?

Discuss this all up front so you feel comfortable in your own home.

Give and Take

The following are ten thoughts on common roommate issues mentioned here.

" Even after I talked to her about it, my roommate always listened to my phone messages or "forgot" to give me messages. I finally told my friends to stop leaving messages and just call back until I answered. "
—**Film Studies Major, Carleton College**

" I had a lot of roommates, so we put a timer by the phone. We agreed to a time limit for conversations with friends on campus, since you can easily walk over and talk to them. "
—**History Major, College of Charleston**

" I had a lot of friends and wanted to talk to them on the phone. She was always on the phone with her parents. We had to make a phone schedule. "
—**Finance Major, Georgetown University**

" Sharing food is like opening Pandora's box. Once you give someone permission to have one thing, they will continue to take until you lay down the law. "
—**Physics Major, University of California—Davis**

" Roommates do not have the gift of reading your mind. Telepathically screaming at her to stop using all the milk without replacing it won't solve the problem. "
—**English Major, University of California—Santa Barbara**

" We wound up putting our initials on the food we did not want to share. "
—**Journalism Major, George Washington University**

" My freshman roommate would give out the key to our room to random freshmen. I came home around midnight one Saturday night to find a stranger asleep on my bed! I was very upset—I had assumed my roommate would realize that this was off-limits. I guess I shouldn't have assumed anything. "
—**History Major, Boston College**

" I was awakened in the middle of the night to find my roommate's friend standing in the middle of our room totally drunk and out of it. I sat up and yelled at him and made him leave. My roommate apologized for her friend's outrageous behavior, and after that, we agreed to always lock our door at night. "
—**Sociology Major, New York University**

" It is important to always give each other plenty of space and private time, because you can only take so much of living that close with someone—no matter what good friends you are or how well you get along. "
—**Psychology Major, Georgetown University**

" I wish I had made it clear to my roommate never to ask me a million questions about where I have been or what I did. If I wanted him to know everything, I would have told him. "
    —Marketing Major, University of Alabama

MISCELLANEOUS ISSUES

Think that missed phone messages and noisy roommates are the only issues you will face? Here are a few more things to be aware of that could become an issue down the line.

★ Temperature

" A surprising issue that often pops up is at what temperature to keep the thermostat. A room that is kept at a temperature that is far below or above what you are used to can make you miserable. Temperature is one of those things that you can and should compromise on. "
    —Finance Major, University of Florida—Gainesville

★ Smoking

" I was a nonsmoker; she was a smoker. We compromised by agreeing that she could smoke in our room only if she leaned out the window. "
    —Philosophy Major, Antioch College

★ Nudity

 My roommate liked to walk around our room naked.
At first I was kind of weirded out by this, but as time
passed, I got over it and got naked too.
    —**Criminal Justice Major, George Washington University**

★ WE HAVE TO CLEAN IT OURSELVES? ★

The first thing college students learn when they move out
of their parents' houses is, surprisingly, if you don't clean
something, it's actually NOT going to clean itself. And that
means you and your roommate are going to have to take
care of it. You're not going to have a problem if both of you
are superclean or if you both prefer to live like slobs
(hey, we're not here to stop you!). It's when you have a
difference of opinion that the problems begin, and this
chapter is full of advice from students on what to do about it!

My Roommate Is a Slob

Your roommate is messy. Your roommate is dirty. Your
roommate is slovenly. Your roommate is growing new
lifeforms on his side of the room. Some poor students wind
up paired with the cleaning impaired! Just as with many

other roommate issues, it's best to deal with cleaning problems right away. Here's how to get out of the mess:

★ **Start slowly and with humor.** If your roommate's dirty laundry covers the room, ask him what color the floor is—it's been so long since you've seen it! Sometimes a gentle reminder is all it takes to kick-start someone into action.

★ **If subtle hints aren't doing the trick, speak up.** Come right out and say the knife permanently stuck to the floor with dried peanut butter bothers you. The trick is to blame the mess, not your roommate personally. Don't call her a "disgusting slob." Instead say you are having trouble breathing because her sheets haven't been changed in six months.

★ **Don't clean in private.** If you do, your roommate may be tempted to believe you have a magical relationship with the cleaning fairy. Make sure your roommate is home when you scrub down your half of the room. Midway through your scrub-fest, turn to your roomie and ask if she wants to borrow your bottle of cleaning spray 'cause you're happy to share.

★ **Be prepared to compromise.** If you are an obsessive cleaner/organizer, realize that your behavior is your choice. Your roommate may be happy living among clutter. Just ask that the mess stays on the other side of the room.

★ **If the room gets unhygienic and your room-mate won't lift a dust rag, it's time to visit your RA.** Sometimes a neutral third party can help convince your roommate to clear away the clutter.

Dealing with "Cleaning Allergies"

What do you think about these ten thoughts from students?

" My roommate's favorite quote was 'A clean room is a sign of a misspent life.' "
—**Economics Major, Tufts University**

" It's easy to become messy when your roommate is as well. Stop it before it starts! "
—**Industrial and Labor Relations Major, Cornell University**

" She kept leaving old food out. When I got sick of throwing it away for her all the time, I would leave it on her bed. "
—**Communications Major, University of Colorado—Boulder**

" If my roommate's side of the room was clean and I didn't have the time or energy to clean my side, I hid my mess so she wouldn't have to look at it. "
—Philosophy and Legal Studies Major, Hamline University

" It is helpful to have a schedule of cleaning and chores before things get out of hand. You start the year off saying everyone will do his part and clean up after himself, but after a few weeks the place is a mess and everyone blames someone else. "
—Government Major, Connecticut College

" I feel bad because I never washed the dishes that my roommate brought. Halfway through the year we invested in disposable dishes and utensils, and then we got along so much better. "
—Psychology Major, Saint Leo University

" Sometimes you might have to remind your roommates that they need to mop the floor if you've done it three times and they never have. As long as you act like it's no big deal and you're asking—not telling—people will be okay with it. "
—Psychology Major, University of California—San Diego

" I was a bit of a neat freak, and she wasn't at all. We quickly learned to ignore each other's living spaces. We weren't there to be each other's moms—we were there to be friends. "

—**Communications Major, College of Charleston**

" I don't think my roommate minded all my clutter, and I always made sure to tidy up before her mother came to visit, which was the only time she really seemed to care. "

—**Geography Major, Queen's University**

" Halfway through the year, I found a pile of dirty, moldy dishes stashed under her bed! "

—**Anthropology Major, Kent State University**

BEYOND MAKING YOUR BED

Some students like to keep the cleaning rules simple, like "Make your bed every day." While this may work in the short term, eventually you and your roommate are doing to have to do some real cleaning. Here are some supplies that will help keep your room clean and fresh:

★ Baking soda (a great deodorizer)

★ A dust mop (for when your TV is so dusty it looks like a black-and-white screen)

★ Disinfectant wipes (these make it so easy you don't have an excuse not to clean)

★ Mini vacuum cleaner (perfect for cleaning up crumbs and dust bunnies!)

★ SHARE AND SHARE ALIKE ★

Back in preschool, you were forced to share. Well, now you're an adult (almost) and you shouldn't have to share. Should you? Well, yes and no.

Most people don't mind lending you a pencil or a tissue, but when it comes to bigger or more personal items, property rules should be established from the start. Many roommate problems start with miscommunication over sharing.

Here are some general rules to keep in mind when you choose to share:

★ **If you have certain ways you want your property to be treated, let your roommate know.** If you don't want your iPod used as a doorstop, ask your roommate to please leave it where she found it.

★ **If you borrow something, always return it promptly in the same condition that you received it.** Get real—there is no way your roommate is going to believe the tire was flat on her bike before she lent to it you. Get it fixed. And, yes, she will miss it if you keep riding it to class every day this month!

★ **Be honest about what you borrow from your roommate or if you lost or broke something.** If you break it, replace it. If you have absolutely no idea where you left his football after that awesome game in the snow, it's time to go shopping. That ball is not turning up after the first thaw!

★ **Restock supplies and do it ASAP.** If you used the last tissue, buy another box (even two) before your roommate gets a nasty cold and has to use your T-shirt to blow her nose.

★ **Always ask first.** Just because you share the room does not automatically give you the right to share everything IN the room. Never assume that what is your roommate's is by proxy yours as well. Sure, all your towels are damp and dirty and your roommate's towels are clean, fluffy, and folded. That does not mean you are allowed to filch one.

Other Sharing Rules to Live By

We asked many, many students about their experiences with sharing, and two things stood out. First, if (and that's a BIG if) you choose to share clothes, be sure there are rules in place:

★ **Make it known from the start what clothes are off-limits and which ones are up for grabs.** Don't assume that if a never-been-worn sweater still has a tag on it, your roommate will know that she can't borrow it.

★ **If your roommate lets you borrow something and you get a stain on it, wash it (and fold it!) before you return it.** Check the label first, though. If it says "dry-clean only," you'll need to shell out a few bucks and get it dry-cleaned.

★ **If you ruin whatever clothing your roommate let you borrow, replace it immediately or offer to pay for it.** It doesn't matter if it wasn't your fault— if you borrowed the clothing, you are responsible.

★ **Return whatever you borrow.** Sure, your roommate said you can wear her fleece pullover whenever you want, but that does not mean it should reside in your closet.

★ **Don't treat your roommate's closet like a store.**
If you have no more white T-shirts, don't spend
the rest of the year borrowing your roommate's.
Go out and buy your own.

But the overwhelming advice we heard from every student on
where to absolutely draw the line is on sharing a computer.
All you have to imagine is either one of you accidentally
erasing a semester's worth of work or each having a huge
paper due on the same day to realize that this is a BIG
mistake. Save yourself the hassle and use the computer lab
on campus or bring your own computer.

Does Sharing Work?

It can work, but if you're not entirely convinced, read these
ten thoughts from students about how sharing can be a
blessing or a nightmare.

" A sharing policy is good, but a "take-anything-when-
you-need-it" policy can lead to unspoken resentment if
one roommate feels taken advantage of. "
    —Economics Major, Brandeis University

" The secret to sharing successfully is to treat each other's belongings as if they were your own. "
—English Major, University of North Carolina—Chapel Hill

" My roommate and I successfully shared food. It's a waste to have multiples of things like milk and butter. "
—Economics Major, Michigan State University—East Lansing

" My roommate and I did laundry together to save quarters. "
—Political Science Major, Texas A&M University—College Station

" I know it sounds like a good idea in the beginning to share clothes—especially for girls—but if something ever happens to your roommate's favorite sweater while you are wearing it, the tension in the room skyrockets! "
—Economics Major, Bucknell University

" Do not share your clothes with your roommate without a clear policy! You risk having your clothes mysteriously disappear—and you may see other people in your dorm wearing them as well. "
—Art History Major, University of Maryland—College Park

" It's easy to think that sharing a roommate's computer will be fine, but usually deadlines for midterms and finals fall at the same point in the year for everybody. **"**
—Ethics Major, Yale University

" If one roommate has a computer and the other does not, there should be an agreement from the get-go about usage times or whether it will be shared at all. **"**
—Biology Major, Smith College

" Never share anything you cannot afford to replace yourself—just in case your roommate refuses to replace it. **"**
—Government Major, Connecticut College

" I recommend that you do not share your car—my roommate racked up quite a few parking tickets on mine. **"**
—Business Management Major, California State University

★ SURVIVING THE DORM ★

Other than a stint in prison (and we hope this never happens to you), it's unlikely that you will live in a building crammed with so many people in a small space ever again. It will take some getting used to, and it will take some sage advice for you to know how best to deal with life in a dorm. Here are ten thoughts from students on what they wish they had known before they moved in.

" Realize that if you can make it through one year in the smallest room ever, you will appreciate every other place you live for the rest of your life. "
        —**Marketing Major, University of Notre Dame**

" Find someplace you can call your own. Suddenly you are living with a bunch of kids your age, none of who really know you. It can be overwhelming. Putting aside personal time and space becomes really important to your happiness. "
        —**English/French Major, Cornell University**

" Be open and talk to your hall mates. Suppressing inhibitions and fears of talking to the 'stranger next door' is key to adjusting to dorm life, particularly when homesickness rears its head. "
        —**Sociology/Political Science Major, State University of New York—Buffalo**

" Make friends inside the hall, but get involved in clubs so you are out and about a lot, and coming home feels like home—not a prison where you spend all your time. "
    —**Sociology/Family Studies and Human Development Major, University of Arizona**

" Make friends on your hall. If you do, you will always be guaranteed to have someone to go to dinner with and possibly find a new roommate for next year. "
    —**Biology and Nutrition Major, Pennsylvania State University**

" Have friends outside your dorm. Dorms, by the second month of school, tend to turn into soap operas. You need a place where you can go hang out with friends who don't live with you. "
    —**Political Science Major, St. Joseph's University**

" Stay away from 'hall-cest' (hooking up with/dating someone in the same hall or dorm as you) if your hall is small. You will feel like you are married, because that person is always there!!!! And it will be bad if you break up in the middle of the year, 'cause you will see the person all the time!!! "
    —**Biology Major, Oberlin College**

" Don't leave your laundry sitting in the machines for hours. People WILL take your wet clothes out of the washers and leave them on the floor. "
—**English Major, Fordham University**

" Wash your hands often. Although it sounds silly, it will help you stay healthy when others around you get sick. "
—**Health and Society Major, University of Rochester**

" Pack a fan. Dorm rooms are stifling! "
—**Psychology Major, University of Alabama—Tuscaloosa**

So you now have a survival guide to living in the dorms. Now it's time to talk about why you're really at college (no, not the prospect of nightly parties!): studying. You may think that your high school experience is enough to get you through, but if you have the chance to get some expert advice, why not?!? Chapter 3 has all you need to know.

Yes, You Are There to Study

It is shocking how easy it is to forget the real reason you are off to college. All this talk about dorms, roommates, and socializing probably hasn't helped keep your mind on track to the fact that what you're actually doing is going to school.

We already covered the basic differences between high school and college in Chapter 1, and I'm sure you're aware that your life as a student will change. So, in this chapter, we seasoned graduates will offer you a 101 course on the main aspects of your college education: time management, studying, tests and papers, professors, and of course, courses and majors. ★

Our best general advice we can give is to be proactive. This is your education, so you can get as much or as little out of it as you put into it. And don't simply read this chapter and think you are an expert. Really get to know your school—what your professors are like, what your class schedule will be, what majors interest you right now (because, believe us, your interests will change!). Every school is different, and there's a reason you chose this one. Just remind yourself again what that reason is.

★ TIME MANAGEMENT ★

It is definitely worth repeating here that a major change from high school to college is your schedule. Gone are the days when you have to be in homeroom by 8:00 AM, eat lunch at 12:30 every day, and aren't allowed to have your own life until the final bell rings at 3:00 PM. When you start college, you'll be able to create your own schedule based on the number of classes you will have. And while it may seem like heaven on earth to only take one or two classes per day, you have to understand the additional, unwritten requests for your time.

Take homework, for example. In high school, you perhaps spent two to three hours per week studying outside your regular school day. Well, in college, it's not unreasonable to spend that same amount of time each week studying and preparing for *each class* you take! And that doesn't even take into account busier times such as during midterms and final exams. Your free time actually comes at a cost.

In addition, since there is no parent to stand over your shoulder every night to check your homework, you've got to establish and maintain a discipline to complete all of your assignments. Even if there are no pop quizzes to make sure that you've done the reading, you are expected to know the information at some point—whether it's for writing a term paper or completing your final exam.

So how do you avoid temptation to rush back from class to watch Oprah or go play Ultimate Frisbee? Well, that's really up to you. A good rule is to devote a certain portion of your day to your schoolwork—for example, no weekday parties, or complete all your homework by 5:00 PM so that you have the rest of the day off. Once you get in a routine or a schedule that works well for you, stick to it. Your friends will learn not to bother you when you are in the library on Saturday mornings or not to tempt you with a frat party on a Tuesday night.

ARE YOU A MORNING PERSON?

When most students are creating their schedules, they avoid morning classes like the plague. However, if you are one of those people who would rather have all their classes over by 2:00 PM, make it happen.

Although I wasn't a morning person, I tended to seek out the early section of classes. It helped me minimize the temptation to go out on weeknights, and it also meant that my day was over when other students were just getting up for their first class.

Making the Most of Your "Free" Time

Here are ten thoughts from students who learned, sometimes the hard way, how to manage their time and do their best academically.

" It's going to seem like you have a lot of free time because you are only in class for three to four hours a day. When midterms come around, however, you will realize what you were supposed to be doing during that 'free time.' "
—Biology Major, College of Charleston

" You should expect to spend the same amount of time studying as you spend in class. And don't think that weekends are for hanging around; they are for studying during the day and having fun at night! "
—Government Major, University of Virginia

" I make a schedule and tell myself that I have to get through a certain amount of work before I go to bed each night. It gets easier as you get older, because everyone's majors get more demanding, so there are fewer people to fool around with. "
—Biology Major, Bucknell University

" Just planning out your day or week can be a great help because it lets you know when you have meetings, when you have projects due, and also when you have time to hang out with your friends. "
—Environmental Studies Major, Emory & Henry College

" I always find it helpful to have a calendar and write down when everything is due. That way you're not waiting until the last minute to finish assignments, especially when you have multiple assignments due on one day or in one week. "
—**Near Eastern and Judaic Studies Major, Brandeis University**

" You cannot leave anything till the last minute. For tests, begin reviewing a few days in advance. For papers, the amount of time depends on the length of the paper, but leave yourself enough time to do a good outline, rough draft, and final version. "
—**Government Major, Dartmouth College**

" It sounds like a lot of work, but it really is important to study at least a little bit every day. If you study for a hard class every day, you won't need to cram for a test, and you will have a much better understanding of the class material. "
—**Biomedical Sciences Major, Marquette University**

" Don't let things slide—you can't make up an entire semester's worth of work the night before a final. "
—**Journalism/Philosophy Major, Syracuse University**

" Make a schedule and stick to it. It was not until my senior year when I had a full course load, GREs, grad school applications, and a senior thesis to write, all in one semester, that I really learned how helpful this can be. It is an amazing lifesaver. You get enough done and you keep moving rather than getting bogged down and overwhelmed. "
—**Sociology Major, Mills College**

" It's really not all that hard to balance work and play. Just do your work before you play, and if you don't get it done, then you can't play! Your GPA might be your saving grace someday when applying to law school, med school, or grad school. You might have an average/mediocre LSAT score, but an amazing GPA speaks loud and clear about what a hard worker and a talented student you really are. "
—**Government Major, Lafayette College**

★ THE ART OF STUDYING ★

Here's a shocking revelation: studying is not something students like to do. As a result, many students are actually not very good at it. Although all-nighters and cramming work is for some of you, others realize that this is not the ideal way to go. So let's take some time to review some of the methods that will help you improve your study skills.

Bits and Pieces

Let's say you're glancing over your syllabus for your first class of the day. Instead of seeing what your assignments are for each class period, you skip right to the end and see ALL the information that will be tested on the final exam. Your heart starts racing, your mind goes blank—in a matter of seconds, you have convinced yourself that you will fail this class.

Take the syllabus for what it is . . . a daily or weekly break-down of all the information covered in the entire course. You should never try to set a goal such as, "Read all of Psychology 101 textbook this Saturday." Instead, work along with the syl-labus so that your goals are much more manageable. Smaller, more realistic goals will keep you on track and prevent those moments of utter panic.

Location, Location, Location

Where do you study best? Lying on your bed? Tucked in the corner of a bustling coffee shop? Hunched over in the silent stacks of the main library? Take a moment to think of where you get your best studying done. When you find a place that works for you (and that has plenty of light to read by), make that your official study space.

Peace and Quiet?

If you need some sort of background noise, try bringing along your music player with headphones or try studying in the student center. If absolute silence works for you, the library is probably your best option. Find the atmosphere that helps you stay focused for long hours of studying.

The Right Time of Day

No matter how many times you tell yourself you will get up and study before your first class, that snooze button on your alarm clock usually dictates your schedule. If your brain works best late at night, plan to do your studying then. If you get drowsy after a meal, don't even think about studying after lunch. Listen to your body and your mind about when the best time of day is for you to study.

Study Groups

Peer pressure is a great motivator, and as the old saying goes, misery loves company. If you have a particularly challenging course, try organizing a study group. Each member of the group will bring particular strengths, and you can rely on a particularly knowledgeable group member to help reinforce the lesson. However, when selecting your group, be sure that they are there to study, not to socialize!

Treat Yourself!

One way to stay motivated when you think you can't read another word is to set up a rewards system. Make a bargain with yourself—"If I study one more hour, I can go down the hall to watch this week's episode of *Grey's Anatomy*." or "If I can get 100 pages of reading done by Friday, I'll treat myself to breakfast at my favorite diner on Sunday." If you know that something positive (other than a decent grade) will come from your hard work, it will be easier to stay on task.

Failure Is Not an Option

Here are ten thoughts from students about ways to make studying slightly less painful.

" If the thought of the sterile and prisonlike library dissuaded me from my study plans, I would bring the books to a cozy coffee shop and make a point of enjoying it. "
—International Relations Major, Brown University

" I'd go to a 24-hour diner far away from campus where I knew nobody else would be and stay til the sun came up. "
—Political Science Major, University of California—San Diego

" I locked myself in the silent floors of the library. Once you get a couple of bad grades, it's not hard to force yourself to sit down and work. "
—**Government Major, University of Virginia**

" I went to the library or study lounge . . . when people around you are studying, it's easier to get motivated. "
—**English/American Studies Major, University of Notre Dame**

" Study groups were very beneficial to me since I tend to procrastinate when I'm by myself. Meeting with a group of classmates regularly keeps you on your toes because you never want to be the freeloader. "
—**Microbiology/Sociology Major, University of Oklahoma**

" I made sure that I had incentives like, 'once I finish this I can take a break . . .' to get ice cream, watch a movie, or anything that sounded appealing. "
—**Pre-Law, University of Illinois—Urbana-Champaign**

" I make a schedule with check boxes and check off each of the boxes as I finish my tasks. It always feels very rewarding to cross off something from my list! "
—**Legal Studies/Sociology Major, University of Wisconsin**

" Just thinking that my parents are shelling out gobs and gobs of money for me to be here is motivation enough. I don't want to have to deal with Dad—minus $25,000—when I get a D. "

—Chemical Engineering Major, University of Virginia

" I forced myself to face the prospect of failing and hated it so much that I just knew I had to sit and get through my studies. "

—Psychology Major, University of Pennsylvania

" Throw on some sweatpants, turn off your cell phone, and get lost in the library. "

—Political Science/Chinese Language Major, University of California—Irvine

★ TESTS AND PAPERS ★

You won't be on campus long before you realize how the campus vibe changes when it comes time for tests and papers. The libraries are busier, the computer labs are more crowded, and the 24-hour coffee shops increase their staff to keep up with the demand. The main thing to do is to accept that tests and papers are a reality. Pretending those looming exam dates are still far off won't help. Put all major assignments on your calendar or in your PDA so that you can prepare well in advance.

One of the biggest causes of stress over tests and papers is the unknown. Make sure you know all the details. Like this . . .

For Tests:

★ Is it multiple-choice? Short-answer? Essay question? Open book? Closed book?

★ What specific chapters or concepts does it cover?

★ How is it graded?

★ How much of your final grade does it account for?

★ Is there any possibility to retake the test?

For Papers:

★ Is it open-ended or is the topic assigned?

★ Is outside research required?

★ How many pages should it be? How many words should it be?

★ How should it be formatted? Margins? Font size? Cover page?

★ Are footnotes/endnotes required?

★ Does it require a bibliography?

★ How is it graded?

★ How much of your final grade does it account for?

★ Do you have the opportunity to submit a first draft?

You will find that when you are completely informed about what is expected of you, you can set specific goals and prepare to do your best.

It's All in the Preparation

Here are ten thoughts on the best way to handle tests and papers in college.

" 'Overprepare' for your first round of tests. "
— **Political Science Major, Texas A&M University**

" Don't stress too much. I had friends freshman year who nearly had nervous breakdowns, convincing themselves that every test would make or break the rest of their lives. "
— **Anthropology Major, University of Vermont**

" The first college exam you take is most likely going to kill you. It's normal. You use that painful realization and channel it into motivation to prepare for the next one. "
— **Biology/Chemistry Major, Houston Baptist University**

" Go to class. Going to the lectures will let you know exactly what information is important. If you don't go to class, you are on your own. I also recommend recopying lecture notes. I was given this tip at college orientation, and it worked for me. "
—**Government and Politics Major, University of Maryland— College Park**

" I think one of the most important things that I've learned is to really listen and understand during lectures. Don't just copy exactly what the professor says or writes, paraphrase to ensure your understanding. It really cuts down on time spent being confused later when you sit down and try to relearn your notes. "
—**Biology Major, University of California—San Diego**

" Learn how to write during your first semester in college. Invest time in your freshman writing course! Writing in college is completely different from in high school, and the most common comments from freshmen are about how their high school teachers loved their writing, but now in college they are doing horribly on their writing assignments. "
—**Speech Pathology Major, Towson University**

" Figure out how to write a college paper as soon as possible. This includes actually coming up with something interesting/original to say, picking out quotes from the text, and for extra pizzazz, adding quotes from outside sources and using beautiful vocabulary and sentence structure. "
—**Ethnic Studies/History Major, Brown University**

" Utilize the writing center on your campus. Those people have experience in writing and can definitely help you improve your writing skills and papers. Also, you should ask for help from teachers. Ask them for examples of what they're looking for ("So what would an A paper look like?"). "
—**Psychology Major, University of Alabama**

" Set your own deadline for three to five days before the paper is actually due. On that day have a final draft completed. Leave it alone for a day or two and then come back to it. This will give you perspective on your own work and help you avoid writing the paper all on the last night. "
—**Biopsychology Major, University of Michigan**

" Never turn in a paper that hasn't been proofread by two or three people. You may think you're error-free, but you'll be surprised by what you overlooked the night before while dozing off at the computer. "
—**English Major, Morehouse College**

★ PROFESSORS ★

We won't lie to you—you're more likely to remember the name of the guy who streaked during graduation or the name of the fraternity with the best parties than you are to remember who taught your introductory-level English class. But just because every professor isn't the most memorable does not mean that all professors should be overlooked. In fact, professors are an integral part of your college experience because you will learn from them, seek advice from them, and try to earn the best grade you can from them.

If it helps, remind yourself that your professors were once students themselves. They obviously have experience working with students, and despite what you may think, they are not there to fail you or make your college experience miserable. Be proactive and get to know them—and you'll be amazed how much you will actually learn.

LEARN TO READ THE SIGNS

Among all professors there are the outstanding ones, and the ones who would rather give you an F than actually take the time to help you learn (you know who they are!). Talk to previous students who have had certain professors before. If you notice a class is immediately full semester after semester, you can guess that the professor is one of the great ones. If you're constantly hearing complaints like "BORING!", then try to find another professor who teaches that course.

Don't Be Quick to Judge

If you are totally freaked out about talking one-on-one with your professor, take this advice from students who have felt the same way. Here are ten thoughts about what professors are really like.

" College professors are normal people. Some are kind, some are jerks, some are smart, some are brilliant, some are awful teachers, some are superb instructors. And you have to accept that and approach them accordingly. TAs are mutants; cross your fingers and hope they're normal. "

—Philosophy Major, Northwestern University

" Professors and teacher's assistants genuinely care that you're learning. They're not there to ruin your life (a misconception we all had in high school). They're there because they are passionate about what they're teaching you, and they want you to see why they love what they're teaching. Show them that you care about what you're learning, not just to get a good grade but because you're interested in the subject. "

—Biometry and Statistics Major, Cornell University

" Most professors truly want to help you; however there are those who seem like they want nothing more than to watch you fail. Don't let those professors get you down. Work harder to succeed despite them. Trust me, it feels good when you do. "
—**Biology Major, Mary Washington College**

" Be early to class—walking in late is very rude. I was amazed at how many times I saw students walk in late right in front of a professor while she was lecturing. The professor didn't like this at all. It is also rude to leave class before the lecture is over. "
—**Economics/Government and Politics Major, University of Maryland—College Park**

" If you aren't going to be in class, make it a point to write a quick e-mail to your professor. And when you get back to class, make it a point to talk to the professor about what you have missed and explain that you are concerned about falling behind. They will get to know your name, and they will see that you are truly concerned about the course. "
—**English Major, George Mason University**

" Never miss an opportunity to ask other students which professors they have taken classes from and what they thought about the professors and the classes. A good professor is the most important factor in choosing classes, and information from former students is the most valuable resource when choosing classes. "
—**Political Science Major, University of California—San Diego**

" Professors and TAs are pretty accommodating, so make sure that you have good communications with them. They are not mind readers so you have to take the initiative and explain your problem, and most of the time you will be pleased with the result! "
—**Biochemistry Major, Rutgers University**

" Just because they're great lecturers doesn't mean they have great people skills. And just because they're bad lecturers doesn't mean they have bad people skills. "
—**Biology Major, University of California—San Diego**

" Show you're trying, even if it's an e-mail before a test asking a question you already know the answer to. They love feeling like they are important and actually teaching you things outside of the classroom. "
—**Sociology/Family Studies and Human Development Major, University of Arizona**

" If you show enthusiasm in your instructor's fields or in what they are teaching you, then it will be easy to get their attention. Sit up in front and right in the middle of the lecture hall. If you are really interested in the subject or lecture, use physical communication to show it. Smile and nod your head to show you understand what is being said. Although a freshman might not think it's important for the lecturer to know that she exists, establishing a relationship with one's instructors is very important, and it will pay off tremendously once the time comes to ask those instructors for letters of recommendation to get into grad school. "

—**Psychology/Social Behavior Major, University of California—Irvine**

★ COURSES AND MAJORS ★

Depending on where you go to school, you could have a wide variety of courses and majors to choose from. You may think that after applying to college and being accepted that you are done with filling out forms and making decisions. However, enrolling and actually creating your schedule are absolutely necessary. Most likely, during your freshman year you will have to take a majority of required classes (English, math, etc.), but take the time to review the online or printed course book offered by your school. Until you familiarize yourself with all your options, you might not even know what courses you really want or need to take.

Finally, never underestimate the help you can get from your academic advisor. Your advisor will be a great resource for planning your schedule so that you can take the classes you want and the classes you need—and do it all in four year's time.

PLAY THE WAITING GAME

At most schools, you don't have to declare your major until the end of your sophomore year. For this reason, you should avoid the temptation to rush your decision and declare a major until you are really, *really* certain what you want to study. It could actually be more efficient to remain "undecided" than to declare a major only to have to switch it later and start over with prerequisite courses. Take our advice and take the time that is available to make your decision.

No Really, What Courses Should I Take?

Let's go right to the source. Here are ten thoughts from students on what courses and majors mean to your college career.

" I made the mistake of taking all of my general requirements in the first two years, and when I became an
upperclassman, I was stuck with all my high-level
classes at once. It is difficult to raise your GPA when you
have all biology classes in one quarter. I should have
consulted my advisor more, but I thought I knew what I
was doing on my own. "
    —**Biology Major, Ohio State University**

" Think about how much time you have between classes
and other commitments rather than trying to always end
up with four-day weekends. You can use this time to
study, instead of wasting four days trying to force yourself to study. This way you have a ready-made study
schedule. "
    —**Economics Major, State University of New York—
    Stony Brook**

" I came into college as a business major because I
thought it was a good route to take. Wrong! I ended up
taking classes I wasn't interested in, and therefore I did
horribly, which killed my GPA. So if you're not sure what
you want to do, there's nothing wrong with saying that
your major is 'Undecided.' "
    —**Family Studies Major, Miami University**

" Have a desire to learn the subject matter. If you don't like the topic, it doesn't matter how good the teacher is—you won't get anything out of doing the work. "
    —**Film Major, Northwestern University**

" Once you figure out your major, take the requisite courses. I could have graduated early, but I was not able to enroll in all of the classes I needed, because in my freshman year I took more of a broad curriculum instead of being more focused on my major. "
    —**International Studies/Russian Major, Johns Hopkins University**

" Find out EXACTLY what your major requires, then meet with an advisor and work out your entire schedule for the next four years. That way you don't end up with tons of useless classes and have to spend five years catching up. "
    —**Political Science Major, University of California—Davis**

" My biggest regret was not having a set direction in college. For the first two years, I had no clue what I wanted to do. By the time I made up my mind, I had to take all my courses for my majors all together. So my last two years were all the difficult courses. "
    —**Economics Major, New York University**

" This is college; find what you love and do it. If you're not sure what you love, maintain variety and you'll find it. "
—Political Science Major, Colorado State University

" I firmly believe that you go to college to grow academically, socially, and individually. Therefore, I think it is imperative to take classes that further your personal interests as much as your academic interests, even if it means you don't graduate within four years. College is supposed to be 'the time of your life,' and you should have no regrets, so indulging your curiosities is as important as fulfilling your academic curriculum—take a history of film class if it pleases your heart. "
—Journalism Major, University of Texas, Austin

" Take classes you'll enjoy. No major is going to prepare you for a job. "
—Film Major, Brigham Young University

There's no doubt that when you look back on your time in college, memories of studying are not going to be in the forefront of your mind. However, it's important to remember that the core of this experience is your education. Never forget that college is both costly and voluntary—if you can't keep up with your studies, there is no obligation for your family or school administrators to keep you there. Enjoy college, but never take it for granted.

Next, we'll face another reality of college: paying for it.

★ F O U R ★

(Not) Going for Broke

You're not even a college student yet, and even so, you have one important lesson committed to memory—money does not grow on trees. As cliché as this saying is, it's true. It's hard work to earn money, and unfortunately, it's incredibly easy to spend.

And of course, if only it were so easy to follow the rule, "Don't spend what you don't have," then NO ONE would be in debt—and you certainly know that isn't true. So in this chapter, I'm going to give you more practical advice. You'll learn some of the (harsh) realities about the costs of going to school as well as some of the other hidden costs behind being a full-time student. ★

But have no fear—this chapter is also full of great ideas for staying out of debt and making the most of every dollar you are lucky enough to get your hands on. You'll even find some creative and, most importantly, safe ways to earn some much needed cash.

★ TUITION IS HOW MUCH?!? ★

Many of us took our high school education for granted. After all, if you went to a public school, your education was paid for! With college, though, there's nothing free about it. Even public schools cost a significant amount—more than $5,000 for tuition each year, not including essentials such as room and board, textbooks, transportation, and other personal expenses. Expect at least triple (more often quadruple!) that amount per year for a private school.

If these numbers freak you out, you need to wholeheartedly adopt the philosophy that this money is an *investment in your future*. Spending thousands of dollars on a four-year education is not the same as spending the same amount on a Ferrari. The money put toward your education actually increases in value once you graduate and apply what you have learned to your new career.

So keep things in perspective. Recognize that the cost is significant—but so is the reward of having a college education.

★ THE MONEY WON'T COME TO YOU ★

It doesn't matter how much money you or your family has; everyone can use a little financial help when paying for college. There are typically four ways to receive money:

- ★ Scholarships
- ★ Grants
- ★ Loans
- ★ Work-study programs

A brief description of these money sources is found here, but also be sure to check out the "Web Resources" section of this chapter for Web sites that will help explain these topics in greater detail.

Scholarships

Many, but not all, scholarships are merit based. That means a certain GPA or skill (for example, music or sports) is enough to qualify you for a scholarship. There are also scholarships that are based on some specific feature of the recipient (for example, a particular cultural or ethnic background).

With all that free money out there, you would think that students would be scrambling for scholarships. The number one reason some scholarships go unclaimed is the students themselves. One reason many students don't apply is before they even do so, they have convinced themselves they would not receive any money. Not applying is the only way to guarantee that you will not receive a scholarship.

But the biggest reason students don't earn scholarships is because they aren't proactive. It bears repeating—the money won't come to you! You have to do your research (um, hello, Google!) and find out what is available.

READ THE FINE PRINT!

Make sure that you fill out all your applications and forms neatly, accurately, and completely. Also, remember that once you have a scholarship, you need to keep up with the specific requirements that it entails. Here are a few questions to keep in mind:

★ Will switching majors affect my eligibility?

★ Is community service required to maintain my scholarship?

★ Can I take time off from school and still have my scholarship when I get back?

★ If I drop a course or decide to take a lighter course load one semester, will I need to get special permission to keep my scholarship?

★ Are any extracurricular activities or sports commitments absolutely required by my scholarship (that is, what happens if I receive a soccer scholarship but decide not to play my sophomore year)?

Source: Kay Peterson, PhD, "Keeping Your Scholarship." *www.fastweb.com*

Grants

Here is where the government, both state and federal, steps in to help students pay for school. There are four major federal grants: the Federal Pell Grant, the Federal Supplemental Educational Opportunity Grant (FSEOG), the Academic Competitiveness Grant, and the National Science and Mathematics Access to Retain Talent (SMART) Grant. Again, you should research these, as well as state grants, to see if you can receive money for school.

There are also a lot of private grants from local organizations, corporations, and even the school you plan to attend. These grants may not cover the entire cost of your education, but you will soon realize that every dollar helps!

Student Loans

What makes loans different from (and seemingly less desirable than) scholarships and grants is that loans have to be repaid. So for every dollar you are loaned, you are going to need to pay that dollar back plus interest. Here is some other helpful information about student loans.

There are two general types of loans: subsidized and unsubsidized. With a subsidized loan, the government pays the interest while you're in college; with an unsubsidized loan, you pay all the interest incurred. To receive a federally subsidized load, you must submit the Free Application for Federal Student Aid (FAFSA)—get used to this acronym, it will come up all the time!

As with scholarships, you must be aware of the requirements and stipulations for your loans (that is, repayment dates and income requirements) and make sure you reapply each year or semester as necessary. Staying on top of the details will save you money and hassle in the long run; otherwise, you could end up with less money than you counted on.

Above all else, keep records of your student loans and file away all the paperwork. This will help you keep track of payment plans and important dates and information that affect your loan.

Work-Study Programs

The work-study program is a popular option among students because it allows them to work (not during class times, of course) to pay for school. Jobs are sometimes on campus (no transportation costs!) or off campus (real-world work experience!). The best source for information on work-study programs will be from the financial aid office at your school.

MAKE FRIENDS WITH THE FINANCIAL AID OFFICE

If the money won't come looking for you, neither will the financial aid office. The employees in this office are professionals and are there specifically to help you navigate the sometimes-murky waters of scholarships, loans, and work-study. If you are completely lost and don't know where else to turn, this should be your first destination.

Web Resources: We Googled It for You

www.ed.gov

From this Web site, you can go to "Students" then "Find and Pay for College." Here you will find information about federal loans directly from the source. You can even complete your FAFSA form online.

www.adventuresineducation.org

This Web site has detailed explanations about scholarships, loans, grants, and work-study programs. You can search scholarships; find a financial aid application calendar; or, from the "High School Student" platform, you can learn exactly how to apply for financial aid.

www.collegeboard.com

You might remember this site from when you were taking the SATs. You can also search for scholarships, compare aid awards, and apply for a loan.

www.nelliemae.com

This site shows all the loans available to you and even offers information on how to manage your money. You can learn how to finance your education and even the best ways to use (not abuse) your credit cards.

www.students.gov

Whether you want to calculate how much college is going to cost you or find out how much you'll owe after you graduate, this site has it all. Helpful information and Web links make this an excellent one-stop site.

They've Earned It!

Here are ten thoughts from students about scholarships and other financial aid.

" Try to get scholarships—there is one for everybody. In fact, Joe Smith from Yourtown, USA, can probably find a specialized scholarship for a trumpet player interested in attending culinary school. "
—**Psychology Major, East Tennessee State University**

" Scholarships are definitely the way to go; one would be surprised at how much money there is for students, just waiting to be asked for. "
—**English Major, University of Florida**

" Don't blow your financial aid money on anything but school and books; if you have money left over, save it until the end of the semester when you know you'll get another check for the next semester, and either spend it then or put it in a savings account. "
    —**Journalism Major, University of Texas—Austin**

" I applied for scholarships even when I thought I didn't stand a chance of getting them. And I did get two, so that was worth my time. "
    —**Classical Civilizations Major, University of California—Davis**

" College students should be aware of those obscure, hidden scholarships that are offered by the universities for 'high school seniors.' They will not tell you about them during the recruiting process (that is, high school visits, campus tours, etc.). They basically leave it up to the incoming freshmen to discover them. "
    —**Chemistry Major, University of California—San Diego**

" If you have a choice between accepting more student loans to help out with expenses and credit cards—by all means choose the student loan!! It's a much lower interest rate!! "
    —**Political Science Major, Furman University**

" As a debt-owing college student, I am honestly not opposed to debt. You go into debt to buy a house, so what is wrong with investing in an education? Particularly with subsidized loans—you can't lose. When you can get loans, pay them back after you graduate, when you are working a job that you really want and enjoy and it pays what you are worth. "

—**Biochemistry Major, University of Tennessee—Knoxville**

" I'm paying off my student loans now and have just completed a loan consolidation, taking advantage of the reduced interest rates. As for spending cash while I was in school, I had work-study positions that kept spending money in my pocket. "

—**English/Environmental Studies Major, Alfred University**

" It is very important to make sure that when you are taking out a loan, you choose the box that says subsidized loan. Do not choose the unsubsidized loan. The unsubsidized loan means you pay the interest on the loan, as opposed to the subsidized loan, for which the government will pay the interest. "

—**Women's Studies Major, State University of New York— Purchase**

> " I find that many of my friends accumulated debt without knowing it by accepting the student loans that are offered to them at the beginning of every semester. I wouldn't accept a loan because I would have to pay it back after I graduated. Only take the grants and student work-study, and pay off the rest yourself. That way, you will graduate from college debt-free. "
>
> **—Chemistry Major, George Mason University**

WHERE DOES DEBT COME FROM?

Unfortunately, getting into debt is almost too easy, especially while you're in college and still adjusting to realities such as bills and loans. For example, there are some big-ticket items you might need when you go away to school, and there are all those other "hidden" costs that you might not think about right away.

Big Ticket Item #1: Car

Luckily, not many students need cars. If you live on campus you certainly don't need one, and it's even better when school administrators prevent freshman from having them—it's a no-brainer. However, if you commute to school or if you need a car to navigate the area around your campus, it might be a necessity. Here are some things you should keep in mind:

★ **Maintenance costs.** Don't forget you'll need to set aside money for gas, parking, oil changes, and smog checks.

★ **Insurance.** Payments to keep you covered can take a big chunk out of your budget. Shop around for the lowest insurance rates.

★ **Repairs.** No one likes to think about the car breaking down on the side of the road, but it happens—have some money available in case this happens to you.

Big Ticket Item #2: Computer

Having your own computer can be a real help while you are a student, but don't forget that most schools have well-stocked computer labs that are included in the price of tuition. If you do want (and can afford) your own computer, consider these questions:

★ Laptop or desktop?

★ PC or Mac?

★ What programs will you need?

★ Have I budgeted enough for paper, printer cartridges, and other supplies needed throughout the year?

Think you're safe if you don't need to purchase a car or computer? Not so fast . . .

It All Adds Up

So tuition, room and board, a car, and computer are covered, so that's everything, right? Not even close! To understand all the costs really involved with going to school, you have to account for:

★ Health insurance (Are you covered through your parents? Does your school offer it?)

★ Transportation and travel (Going home for Thanksgiving?)

★ Fraternity or sorority dues (if applicable)

★ Schools supplies (notebooks, pens, paper)

★ Food (not just your meal plan, but everything—snacks, dinners out, coffee on the go)

★ Medicine (contacts? allergy medicine? birth control?)

★ Lab materials (tuition doesn't always cover time and supplies in the lab!)

★ Replacement ID (if you lose your student ID card)

★ Service fees for dropping/adding classes (make sure you know what registration fees are included)

★ Dorm damage (you break it, you buy it!)

More on how to create a budget in a minute. First, let's first hear from some students regarding spending money.

Financial Wizards

Here are ten thoughts from students regarding financial matters.

" Do not get a credit card. I have never had a credit card, and I have made it through four years of college just fine. I have so many friends who ran up their credit card bills and now have problems paying off the charges and the interest. "
—**Business Administration Major, University of Missouri— Columbia**

" Pay off your credit card bill in full every month. If you don't trust yourself not to splurge, use it only for gasoline for your car or something like that. Doing so will build outstanding credit so that when you graduate you can take loans from the bank more easily for 'real-world' things. "
—**Biology/Environmental Studies Major, Washington College**

" Get a part-time job. You appreciate your money when you can translate a dollar into how long you'd have to work to get it. "
—**English Major, Cornell University**

" Just know that there's a difference between 'wants'
and 'needs.' "

—Criminal Justice Major, University of Maryland—College Park

" Take out a certain amount of money each week, and
don't take out any more. If you do that, your money will
last longer, plus you won't keep getting charged all of
those ATM fees. "

—Psychology Major, Hampton University

" Just because you have checks left in your checkbook
doesn't mean that you have money left in your bank
account! "

—Biology Major, University of California—Los Angeles

" Don't be afraid to say no to your friends because you
don't have enough money to do something. Chances are
someone else doesn't have enough money either but is
just too afraid to say so. "

—Biology Major, University of Vermont

" Be realistic and realize that you are in college—you
should be poor! "

—Latin Major, Harvard University

" Have an 'I'm soooo broke' mentality when you're shopping no matter how much money you have—it'll help you decide whether or not you need something. It's OK to spend a little once in a while, but once you're in the red, you're gonna have a hard time digging yourself out. "
—**Materials Science Engineering Major, Arizona State University**

" Live like a student now so that you don't go into debt and have to live like a student after college. "
—**Zoology Major, Brigham Young University**

★ CREATING A BUDGET ★

It's happened to all of us. The waiter just gave you the check for a huge dinner out, or you have a full load of groceries relentlessly moving forward on that conveyor belt, but when you open your wallet, you get that sinking feeling . . . you don't have enough money. Is this bad luck or just a case of bad planning?

Figure out a budgeting system that works for you, especially when you're broke and in college. After all, you can't get by on less if you don't know how much you have or how much you're spending. You're going to need to keep tabs on your money—so you can keep it in your wallet!

The first rule is that you don't have to create a complex budget to get a hold of your finances. Here you will find a sample monthly budget for you to follow. You may think you already know how your money is being spent, but you might be surprised to discover that you're actually spending the bulk of your monthly budget on chocolate cupcakes with sprinkles when you thought it was your textbooks that were doing you in.

Step 1: Add up your monthly income

Your job wages + Money from parents or other outside sources = Total monthly income

Step 2: Add up your monthly expenses

Rent/bills (phone[s], credit card[s], utilities)

+ Books and supplies (notebooks, pens, etc.)

+ Food (including that coffee you pick up on the way to class every day)

+ Entertainment (movies, concerts, dinners out)

+ Emergencies (you'll have to gauge how much extra money you will need to handle any unforeseen expenses that may arise)

+ Miscellaneous (all those items that other people might not need, but you will)

= Total monthly expenses

Subtract your expenses from your income. If you get a negative number, then you're in trouble! Find a way to cut your expenses before you end up flat broke. If you're feeling uninspired (math in any form does that to me!), keep reading to hear what actual students do to budget their money.

When Budgets Meet Reality

Here are ten thoughts from students who created (and sometimes ignored) their budgets.

" Here's my budget: I simply live cheap, eat cheap, and play cheap. "
—**Political Science Major, University of Wisconsin—Madison**

" My roommate and I decided that we would share expenses for groceries. This started out as a good idea, but because we never set guidelines for expenses, my half of the groceries was always way out of my budget. Be sure to set guidelines. "
—**Sociology Major, Marquette University**

" I did a horrible job of budgeting. I have a great collection of DVDs that I acquired in college—about 200 or 300 of them. If I bought them for 15 bucks a pop, that's a lot of money I spent. And now I think, wow, I wish I had that money back, and why do I have a *The Wedding Planner* DVD? "
—**Political Science Major, University of California—Los Angeles**

" My checkbook is my budget. I subtract all known monthly bills from my overall amount at the beginning of the month, and then I know how much I have to spend on other things. "
—**Literature/Writing Major, University of California—San Diego**

" I calculate my main expenses (car payment, insurance, cell phone bill, bank service fee, estimate of gas) for each month and separate that amount from the rest of my money. Then I make sure to keep track of my balance. "
—**Interdisciplinary Studies Major, University of Texas— San Antonio**

" My budget includes a 'money for a rainy day' system: I take about $20 to $40, put it in an envelope in my desk drawer, and 'forget' about it. Every chance I get, I put in a little more, but no more than $100. Once I get up to $100, I know that I can spend it on some much-needed items or use it in case of an emergency. "
—**Pre-Medicine Major, El Paso Community College**

" My parents and I sat down at the beginning of the fall semester and decided my budget—in other words, how much money I need for the entire year (rent, bills, food, miscellaneous). Then we broke it up into 24 'paychecks' that get directly deposited into my account on the 1st and the 14th of every month. It's like having a job, without working. Some months the money is more than enough (when bills are lower), but some months it's really not enough, so I just have to manage really well then. "

—**Government Major, University of Texas—Austin**

" My budget works like this: I divide my paycheck into thirds. The first section is for savings, the second is for bills, and the third is for going out and having fun. If there's money left over, I may splurge more that month or opt to save it. "

—**Spanish Major, Rutgers University**

" My only budget plan is to not buy on impulse. That can get you in trouble and leave you with things that you really could have lived without. "

—**Biology Major, Mesa State College**

" The only bad budget is not having one at all! "

—**Anthropology Major, Emory University**

BANKING 101

Whether you use your account from back home or you open a new account at school, here are some things to consider:

★ Does your bank have low required minimum balances? To maintain some accounts you have to have a certain amount of money in them at all times. Find out the minimum balance for each bank you are considering.

★ Does your bank have easy access to ATMs? Don't count on yourself to be responsible about walking the extra ten blocks to your bank's no-fee ATM if there are other ATMs close by.

★ Does your bank have direct deposit options? This allows your paycheck to be transferred directly into your account without your having to physically deposit it. If you are earning a paycheck or if your parents will be making deposits to your account, this is a great time saver.

★ Does your bank offer overdraft protection? This is a credit line of sorts that the bank gives you (usually a couple hundred dollars) to avoid negative reporting on your credit history if you dip below your balance. Keep in mind that this is money you have to pay back with heavy interest.

Don't let laziness keep you from finding the bank or credit union that's right for you. Go online and do some research. You can even do your banking online—make payments, check your balance, and view your banking activity all from your computer!

★ STRETCHING YOUR DOLLAR ★

Everyone wants to make their money last, at least through the end of the month. So here are some questions to consider if you still find yourself with low resources before your next paycheck arrives:

★ **Where is most of my money going each month? Can I adjust to spend less in one area?** If you're spending a lot of money ordering pizza, then try to cut back. Stock up on snacks or even frozen meals from the grocery store—you'll also save on delivery costs.

★ **Did I need to buy everything I bought this month upfront? Could I have paced myself better?** If you buy four bags of chips for snacks thinking they will last the entire month, chances are they won't. It's better to buy as you go.

★ **Did I go over budget? If so, how can I cut back next month to make up the difference?** If you notice that your cell phone bill is high, try planning your calls so that you make them during your "free" minutes.

Making the Most of It

Here are ten thoughts from students who knew how to make the most of being broke or how to avoid going broke in the first place.

" We went to Barnes & Noble and sat on their couches and read through comic books and magazines. "
—**Art/Psychology Major, East Carolina University**

" There is always free food around. Go to club or organization meetings that offer free dinner or treats. "
—**Math Major, Carleton College**

" Buy food and make it whenever you can. Make a big meal on Sunday and eat leftovers the rest of the week. "
—**Government Major, University of Virginia**

" Always eat on your meal plan unless it's a special occasion. "
—**English/Psychology Major, University of Michigan— Ann Arbor**

" Learn about all the free perks on campus and cheap discounts you get as a student. Most airlines, restaurants, etc. offer a discount to college students if you show an ID."
—Journalism Major, University of Texas—Austin

" Clip coupons and find free things to do with friends."
—Biology, Bucknell University

" I date on a budget by exploring a state park or heading to the beach. You can save money, get to know each other better, and get some exercise in—all at the same time. And picnics are always romantic!"
—English Major, San Diego State University

" Traveling Monday through Thursday can save you money—off-peak days are generally less expensive."
—Political Science Major, University of California—Los Angeles

" Try to drive at or below the speed limit, if possible. Going slowly will save you money on gas."
—Chemical Engineering Major, University of Kansas

" If you're tight for money, a relaxing spring break doing nothing is just as good. After all, it is called a break. "
—**Biology Major, Mesa State College**

★ SAVVY SHOPPING ★

With the seemingly endless array of online and discount retailers, the good news is this: if someone's got it cheap, someone else has it cheaper. As a new college student, you should also take on the role of comparison shopper. With everything from textbooks, to computers, to furniture, to vacation packages, your mission—should you choose to accept it—is to find the lowest prices and the best deals.

Whether you go online (think eBay, Amazon, Craigslist, and Travelocity) or whether you visit an actual store (Ikea, Target, Linens-n-Things), there are definitely deals to be had. So don't pay full price, look around, and then make plans for what to do with that "leftover" money.

Attention Shoppers!

Even out of college, I pride myself on being a bargain shopper—but there's always someone who has a new, great idea for pinching pennies. Here are ten thoughts from students about the best ways to save money while spending money.

" Once I got my car, I made a point to find the cheapest gas stations in my town and on the way home. Very helpful. "
—**Biology Major, University of California—Davis**

" Shop at the dollar store, at garage sales, and on eBay. "
—**Linguistics Major, Brigham Young University**

" The best time to buy an online airline ticket is around 3 or 4:00 AM. This is because the companies update their systems and lower the prices on tickets that aren't selling. Also, if you can wait, buy tickets that can be used in the next day or two; they are often very cheap. "
—**Biology Major, Carnegie Mellon University**

" If you go to school pretty far away from home like me (I live across the country) and you have to fly, then I'd advise getting tickets two to three months ahead of time so you don't have to pay $500 just to go home. Definitely check into frequent flier programs and family plans (for sharing flier miles). "
—**Criminal Justice Major, Indiana University—Bloomington**

" I bought a train pass that was worth ten one-way trips, so it translated to less money per trip than the usual price. "
—Biology Major, University of California—Davis

" Most fast-food chains are known for their 99-cent menus. These will become one of your best friends. It can make at least three meals out of ten dollars. "
—Business Administration Major, Florida A&M University

" Whenever you go out to shop for anything, you should always ask if there is a student discount. Most people don't ask because they are shy, but most schools either have cards that they give out to students as a proof of membership, or students have to simply show their ID. "
—Math Major, State University of New York—Stony Brook

" If you visit a restaurant frequently, such as a deli, make sure to pick up a punch card so that you can get free items after buying the designated amount of items. "
—Economics Major, University of Kansas—Lawrence

" I use the coupon booklets that are passed out all over campus because a lot of coupons for college students involve restaurants. I also have lots of friends who work in restaurants, so I eat there and get a discount. "
—**Psychology Major, Colorado State University**

" Buy the store brand or generic brand instead of the name brand. You'll save a lot of money. "
—**Political Science Major, University of Oklahoma**

★ AFFORDABLE TRAVEL—NO, REALLY! ★

Whether you need some TLC from your mom or just want to relax and party with your friends, you're going to have to deal with the complications of traveling many times throughout your college years. Whether you get there by bus, train, plane, or car, there are ways to get there for less.

Here are a few suggestions for making sure your travel doesn't wipe out your monthly budget:

★ **Carpool.** If you know people who are headed in the same direction as you, consider taking one car and sharing all the expenses.

★ **Travel packages.** You should definitely be wary of some package deals, but consider booking your flight and hotel together on a trusted travel Web site.

★ **Look for online specials.** Every major airline has its own Web site. You should also check out travel sites such as priceline.com, travelocity.com, expedia.com, or hotels.com.

★ **Book in advance.** You will often find that the closer it comes to peak travel times, the more expensive airfare and hotels become. Book early and save!

Wish You Were Here

Here are ten thoughts from students who opted for budget travel—for better or worse.

" Make sure you really investigate 'all inclusive.' Be sure your deal really includes everything from food to drinks to clubs as well. "
— **Sociology Major, University of Minnesota**

" Always be wary of an ad in the back of a newspaper or on a flyer in a random classroom. I came across a deal for a trip to Cancun. Everything seemed pretty and packaged until I did the research. If it looks too good to be true, it probably is. "

—**Journalism Major, University of Colorado—Boulder**

" I saw a deal that included round-trip airfare plus hotel accommodations to Oahu for only $500. But this one was for real, and I went with a friend and we had an amazing time!! "

—**Political Science Major, University of Oklahoma**

" Acquaint yourself with the foreign students on campus. They may very well invite you to visit them in their home country during breaks, thereby cutting down on accommodation expenses. I have friends in France who stay with me for a week each August and who put me up each year in the heart of Paris! We all win. "

—**Communication Major, Santa Barbara City College**

" Greyhound buses are really cheap and not so bad if you go to school less than five hours from home. Check the schedules and take the express route with fewer stops. Also, buy the student advantage card and use it, or ask for student discounts. "

—**Economics Major, Tufts University**

" Bum rides from other people. Put up signs in the dorms if you're looking to go somewhere; you never know if someone who needs company is heading your way. "

—**Marketing/Graphic Design Major, University of Notre Dame**

" Spring break is for sleep. I am not one of those 'Girls Gone Wild' types. Simply take it easy, go out with friends, and go to the beach if possible. You can gather funds from a few roommates and rent a condo or vacation cottage for the weekend. "

—**English Major, Florida International University**

" I hear about these deals to Cancun and ski resorts. I don't look twice at them, though. Usually, if you're smart, you can create your own spring break deal. That's how a lot of my friends do it. The people who offer the deals are usually a third party and tack their expense into the package. Cut out the middleman and deal directly with the hotels. "

—**Economics Major, University of Texas—Austin**

" I grew up by a spring break hot spot, so I knew all about it. Call hotels or rental agencies about six months to a year in advance. If it is a package deal, try to find someone who has used/done that one before. It is easy to find people to recommend the best hotels, hot spots, and restaurants if they have been there before. "

—**International Studies Major, Emory University**

"" When all else fails, be creative! The best spring breaks happen when you do what you want to do with whom you want to do it. Take a road trip home for free meals and free rooms, or check out all the regional treasures you've never had time to visit before. **""**

—**Italian Studies Major, New York University**

★ SAFE WAYS TO SCORE EXTRA CASH ★

Even the most budget-conscious college student needs to make some fast cash every once in a while. But the real skill in this is being safe and sensible while still being creative enough to make money. Here are some common sense dos and don'ts:

Do:

★ **Try to make money doing something you are good at or have a special skill for.** Tutor math students, offer to fix someone's car, or play live music at your friend's next house party.

★ **Consider selling things you no longer use.** Your fellow students always seek CDs, DVDs, textbooks, clothing, and sports equipment.

★ **Be willing to do something you might not enjoy.** Even if you hate it, you can make money cleaning a friend's house, distributing fliers, or taking on a paper route.

Don't:

★ Do anything illegal or that puts you in any physical danger. Enough said.

I Did It for the Money

Here are ten thoughts from students who found a safe, legal, and effective way to get some much-needed cash.

“ Offer to help clean other friends' houses . . . it's funny how students hate to clean anything! ”
    —Psychology Major, University of California—Davis

“ Car washes. They're the best way to go. ”
    —Biology Major, College of William & Mary

" I got hired as a testing proctor. I can study while I proctor the tests and get paid for doing virtually nothing. "
     —Psychology Major, East Carolina University

" I used to tutor people who desperately needed help on difficult subjects such as chemistry and organic chemistry . . . and sometimes they'd be willing to pay $25 or $30 an hour! "
     —Chemistry Major, University of California—San Diego

" Since I am mechanically inclined, I am able to fix people's cars and get paid for it. "
     —Molecular Cell Biology Major, San Diego State University

" We threw a house party and charged everyone $5. We made a lot of money. This should only be done, of course, when you don't have studying to do and when you can monitor who is coming to your house so that it doesn't get too rowdy! "
     —Biology Major, University of Wisconsin—Milwaukee

" Sometimes I sold my typing skills to guys who
couldn't type. "
—Sociology Major, Marquette University

" I sign up for psychology experiments that pay per hour.
I don't partake in anything that can be harmful. "
—Art History Major, University of California—Davis

" I sold old clothes to a consignment shop. "
—Psychology Major, University of Alabama—Tuscaloosa

" I've done everything from having a garage sale to selling
stuff on eBay! "
—International Studies Major, Emory University

Whew! Hopefully, you've finished this chapter feeling like
there is plenty of hope for financing and enjoying your college experience. It's not all dollar signs and doom, after all.
The final lesson you should take away from this chapter is
that preparing yourself now for financial realities and responsibilities will only make your transition after college even
easier. Get into good financial habits now, and you will thank
yourself later.

In the next chapter, we'll explore more great advice from students and grads on overcoming some nonfinancial problems many students face in college.

When a Friend Is in Need, or You're in Need of a Friend!

I'm not going to lie—going away to school was (at the time) one of the scariest things I had ever done. And the first semester was rough! I would have loved any excuse to go back home and re-enroll in high school. Oddly enough, if you asked me to trade in my life now to go back to college, the answer is YES! Although this seems contradictory, it's really not; college really can be full of the ups and downs that make life what it is—unpredictable.

In this chapter, my fellow graduates will review some of the things that can make college a challenging, but ultimately rewarding, experience. What you have to remember is that most problems have solutions and that, in a few years, the worst of times are likely to be nothing more than long-forgotten memories. ★

Also, please know that you should take the advice in this chapter at face value. Remember that if you or a friend is truly in trouble and don't know where to turn, you should consult the experts: parents, college administrators, advisors, counselors, nurses, or other professionals.

★ MAKING NEW FRIENDS ★

Does it seem like you and your best friend have just always seemed to know each other? Do you even remember a time when you didn't know each other? If you're like most people, we take our friends for granted. We don't remember what it's like not to have a friend or to have to make a new one. With college, all that will change. Unless you go to school with someone you know, that first day you'll be faced with the prospect of meeting many, many students, but more importantly, determining whether you will ultimately call any of those students a friend.

Remember, you have to put yourself out there. Friends aren't going to come to you. You should also learn to develop a sense of true friendship. Lots of people will say they are your friend, but when the chips are down, they might not be around. Choose wisely!

Making Friends 101

Here are ten thoughts from students on how to make new friends when you go away to college.

" The best way to meet people in college is to get involved! Only in college will you find so many young people in one place who all want to meet people with similar interests. "

—Biology/Nutrition Major, Pennsylvania State University

" The first few weeks of school is the time to go to the parties that you normally wouldn't go to . . . that's when everyone goes. Meet people that way; then you can settle into your own little niche. "
—Chemical Engineering Major, University of Virginia

" Meet the people around you in your first year. After that, it keeps getting harder because everyone is already associated with another group of friends. "
—Biology/English Major, Indiana University—Bloomington

" I just said hi and tried to talk to as many people as I could—even if it was just small talk—for the first couple of days, especially people in my dorm or classes. Eventually, you discover who you really enjoy talking to. "
—Sociology Major, University of Hawaii—Manoa

" I met people by talking to anyone and everyone I found remotely interesting in any one of my classes. It may be difficult to do at first, and some of the people you approach may not take to it well, but in the long run it definitely pays off. "
—Psychology Major, Xavier University

" The best way to meet people in college is through study groups and social activities. Always be the person in class that anyone could ask for help in that particular subject, and you will automatically become popular. "
—**English Major, Morehouse College**

" Be outgoing. Be the first one to talk in class when the TA asks you to break into groups. It's easy to stay outgoing when you start, but when you start out quiet, it's tough to switch roles. "
—**Sociology Major, University of Wisconsin—Madison**

" Network. Use people you meet in class and your dorm to meet people they know—try not to pass up the opportunity to go out with a new group of people. "
—**Anthropology Major, University of California—Los Angeles**

" Find people sitting alone in dining halls and, after introducing yourself, sit down to eat with them. "
—**English Major, Cornell University**

" When all else fails, start baking cookies. New friends will flock to you. "
—**Marketing Major, University of Notre Dame**

★ ROOMMATE + YOUR FRIENDS + ROOMMATE'S FRIENDS = TROUBLE ★

Chapter 2 probably offered more than you ever wanted to know about dealing with your roommate. But on the subject of friends, what about your roommate's? Let's say every time you open your door, there they are...sitting on your bed, commenting on your life, or, even worse, completely ignoring you. If you don't like your roommate's friends, here are some suggestions on what to do:

★ **Don't criticize them.** This will only make your roommate defensive and angry with you. Instead, mention in concrete terms why you find it hard to study with them always around or why you'd prefer they not rifle through your things.

★ **Be as friendly as possible.** If you get to know them a little, there might be qualities about them that you actually like, which will make them easier to deal with. For example, you both may love Rocky Road ice cream or cover your ears every time that girl from down the hall sings in the shower.

★ **Tactfully attempt to motivate them to go elsewhere.** Suggest activities that may interest them to leave the room. "Hey, I heard they're giving away free pizza in the dining hall . . ."

On the flip side, maybe you've lucked out and have a huge number of friends, while your roommate doesn't. Even worse, she feels entitled to latch on to your group and never let go. What are you supposed to do when your roommate is always butting in on your plans? Here are some tactful ways to deal with this:

★ **Try to understand where your roommate is coming from.** Maybe she's never had to act independently before because she's always shared a room with a sibling or he's always had a best friend by his side. Don't make fun of your roommate to your friends or try repeatedly to ditch your roommate. The passive-aggressive approach won't work and will only hurt your roommate's feelings.

★ **Set limits.** Make specific plans for the two of you (Monday night at the dining hall or Thursday night for pizza) and then be clear that you have made other plans that don't include your roommate on the other nights.

★ **Be straight with your roommate.** If all else fails, very nicely tell your roommate that the relationship has been a bit intense lately and that you think you'd stay better friends if you each gave the other some space now and then.

Can't We All Just Get Along?

Here are ten thoughts from students about dealing with your roommate's friends or dealing with a roommate who wants to take over your friends.

" I really didn't like my roommate's friends. I told her that I didn't want them around when I was in the room. After that, her friends never hung out in our room, but my roommate and I never had a good relationship, either. I should have handled the situation in a more sensitive manner. "

—Information Technology Major, Rensselaer Polytechnic Institute

" Whenever I came home from class, my roommate was there with her 'clan.' I felt like my privacy was being violated, but I didn't talk to her about it because I didn't want to rock the boat. Instead, I said nothing and avoided being in my own room, which only made me resent her. I should have said something instead of keeping it all inside. "

—History/English Major, McGill University

" My roommate's friends were always around. The best choice I made for my social well-being was joining a sports team and becoming involved in groups on campus. I was so busy that I didn't care about all the people in my room. "
—**Political Science Major, Boston College**

" One of my roommates constantly brought a group of people over—never asking the others if it was an appropriate time. Our walls were really thin and we could hear everything. Eventually my other roommates and I had to talk to her about this, and she agreed to spend equal time at her friends' places. "
—**Psychology Major, University of Alabama**

" I liked my roommate's friend until she started sleeping in our dorm room more often than not. She would eat our food, be in the way, and annoy me when I was studying. I fixed the situation by asking her to contribute to our food fund and be listed on our weekly cleaning tasks. These requests made her realize how much time she was spending in our room—she started coming around a lot less often. "
—**Justice Studies Major, Arizona State University**

" My roommate was younger than I was, and she was very clingy as she tried to adjust to her new lifestyle. She made me feel smothered. I tried to get her to do things—without me—by telling her about events around campus that she was interested in but knew I wasn't! "
—**Sociology Major, Messiah College**

" My freshman roommate was always trying to hang out with me and my friends. She was also scared to sleep in her own bed unless her boyfriend was over. If he wasn't there, she'd crawl into bed with me in the middle of the night! To solve it, I had to talk to her and tell her I liked her, but I needed to have alone time with my friends, and I definitely needed my bed to myself! "
—**Political Science Major, University of Houston**

" My roommate was very clingy. Another one of my friends needed attention all the time. I thought that she would love to have someone who would follow her around and listen to everything she had to say. So I introduced her to my roommate—and just as I predicted—they clicked and became instant friends, and my roommate was able to give me more space. "
—**Justice Studies Major, Arizona State University**

66 The girl I lived with freshman year would invite herself
everywhere with me and my friends. I finally told her that
trying to hang out with us was only keeping her from
meeting people who she would get along better with.
That did the trick!99
—German Major, Emory University

66 Although I was always friendly with my roommate,
I made it very clear that we weren't friends and that I
had my own life to lead.99
—Spanish Major, New York University

★ COMBATING HOMESICKNESS ★

Think you're the only one who misses your high school
friends, your little sister stealing your clothes, or your mom's
apple pie? Think again. Most students experience homesickness at some point during college—but with a little help from
you, it will usually go away! Here's what you can do:

★ **Include him in your activities.** Getting your
roommate involved in a club or an intramural
sport forces him to leave the room and make new
friends.

★ **Suggest that you and your roommate eat dinner together certain nights of the week.** Invite other people from your floor to join you.

★ **Make your own memories.** Is she always talking about the fun times she had with her friends back home? Go out and have fun or be silly together, and then she will be telling her friends back home about the good times that the two of you are having.

★ MORE SERIOUS ISSUES: WHEN LIFE TURNS INTO AN AFTER-SCHOOL SPECIAL ★

One of the signs that you are a good roommate is being able to confront your roommate about a potentially harmful problem. It takes courage to show you care and are concerned. It also helps to handle the problem in an appropriate manner. Whatever the nature of the problem, keep the following advice in mind when approaching your roommate:

★ **Keep it one-on-one.** Ask to talk to your roommate in private. The idea is to lessen the embarrassment and not make your roommate defensive.

★ **Be direct and honest.** Acknowledge that you are aware there is a problem. Explain that you are concerned and are willing to aid your roommate in finding help.

★ **Describe your observations.** If your roommate has been acting strangely or inappropriately, tell her what you have observed in a nonjudgmental manner.

★ **Listen carefully.** Try not to agree or disagree. Stay neutral.

★ **Offer a recommendation.** Tell him where to find professional help. Point out that campus services are nearby and free. Offer to go with him.

★ **Be patient.** At first your roommate may not identify the situation as a problem or may feel embarrassed or threatened by your concern. Be consistent with your support.

★ **You can't do it all.** Realize that it is ultimately your roommate's choice to seek help. No amount of pleading, begging, or preaching by you will make someone do something he doesn't want to do.

Also, one of the most difficult things is admitting that you
yourself have a problem and that you need help. Don't spend
so much time caring for other people that you don't realize
what's going on inside you. Don't be afraid to ask for help,
and don't try to deny that something is wrong.

Depression

Your roommate is seriously bummed out. Maybe her parents
are getting a divorce, or maybe he's failing his classes—whatever the reason, depression is very common among college
students who are living on their own for the first time. In fact,
maybe you are the one who is depressed. Here's what you
need to know: depression is treatable; however, many people
don't seek help because they don't realize that they are clini-
cally depressed. Other people see depression as a sign of
weakness and don't want to reach out for help. Here are
some symptoms to look for in your roommate or in yourself:

★ Persistent sad, anxious, or "empty" demeanor

★ Feelings of hopelessness, pessimism, guilt, and
   worthlessness

★ Loss of interest or pleasure in ordinary activities

★ Sleep disturbances (insomnia or oversleeping)

★ Eating disturbances (increased or decreased
   appetite or weight)

THE DOS AND DON'TS OF HELPING
A ROOMMATE WITH DEPRESSION

Here's some advice for helping a depressed roommate.

Do:

★ Be supportive and listen.

★ Engage him in activities and conversation.

★ Tell your roommate if her behavior frightens you.

★ Encourage him to get treatment. If he won't see a mental health professional, you should see one yourself to gain better insight on the situation.

★ Take any talk of suicide or attempts seriously. Even if you think your friend did it or said something just to get attention, call your school's suicide emergency hotline or call 911.

Don't:

★ Feel that you are responsible for your roommate's depression.

★ Think that you'll be able to fix her life or quickly change her mood. Don't try to talk her out of her depression.

★ Deny or minimize your roommate's pain. Depression is a real problem. Your roommate needs your support.

Source: The National Institute of Mental Health, "What Do These Students Have in Common?" *www.nimh.nih.gov/publicat/students.cfm*

Eating Disorders*

Anorexia and bulimia are both serious eating disorders. People develop eating disorders as a way of dealing with the stresses and pressures of life—often it is a way to exercise control when the rest of life seems out of control.

What is *anorexia*? It is self-imposed starvation. Students with anorexia tend to be obsessed with food yet constantly deny their hunger. Warning signs of anorexia may be if your roommate:

★ is thin and keeps losing weight;

★ obsessively diets even though she is already thin;

★ has a distorted body image (sees herself as fat even though she isn't);

★ exercises all the time;

★ weighs herself several times a day;

★ says she feels chilled even though the temperature is warm; and/or

★ begins to lose her hair.

What is *bulimia*? It is a cycle of out-of-control eating followed by purging (vomiting or excessive use of laxatives or diuretics). Warning signs of bulimia may be if your roommate:

*Adapted from *www.felician.edu/health_counseling/*

★ binge eats;

★ goes to the bathroom frequently after meals;

★ develops swollen glands; and/or

★ appears to go up and down in weight.

THE DOS AND DON'TS OF HELPING A ROOMMATE WITH AN EATING DISORDER

Do:

★ Explain that you are concerned. Give specific examples of behavior that concerns you.

★ Realize that it may take more than one approach before he will agree to get help. Don't give up!

★ Approach the situation in a friendly, laid-back manner. Don't sound as if your mission is to rescue or save her.

Don't:

★ Make your roommate feel ashamed or guilty. Do not use "you" statements like, "You just need to eat." Instead, use "I" statements, like "I'm concerned because you refuse to eat," or "It makes me worried to hear you vomiting so often."

★ Give simple solutions. For example, "Why don't you just start eating again?" Eating disorders are not simple problems with simple remedies.

★ Initiate or participate in conversations about weight and food. When she asks you if she looks fat, don't get sucked in and answer. This legitimizes the topic. Instead, ask why she feels this is important.

★ Try to force her to eat or tempt her with goodies. Eating disorders have nothing to do with food.

★ Compare him with other students. Avoid saying someone is "thin" or "obese."

★ Take on her problem as your own problem. Don't agree to hide her eating disorder. Don't try to become her therapist or make life overly easy for her—this just makes it easier for her to hide from her problems.

★ Expect him to get better overnight. Eating disorders are complex syndromes with many causes. It takes a long time to recover.

Source: *www.nationaleatingdisorders.org*

I'll Be There for You

Here are ten thoughts from students who offer advice on how better to handle problems with homesickness, depression, and eating disorders.

" Sometimes you have to remember that schoolwork can wait and that you need to sit down with your roommate and a mug of hot chocolate NOW. "
—Classical Studies Major, University of Pennsylvania

" Dropping subtle hints does not work. It is best to address issues head on. "
—Mechanical Engineering Major, University of Michigan

" My roommate was lonely being away from home, and I would help by listening to her talk about home. "
—Law Major, Albany Law School

" When one of us got lonely, we'd hit the parties to meet guys. By the next morning, there was enough new drama to forget about being homesick! "
—Anthropology Major, Kent State University

" When my roommate was homesick, I tried to make him laugh. A lighthearted approach can often better contextualize things. "
—English Major, University of California—Davis

" Remember, you are just a college student. Some things are way too big for one person to solve. If the problem is serious, seek outside (professional) help right away. "
—Political Science Major, University of California—Berkeley

" One of my roommates was severely depressed throughout college. It got so bad that I brought her to student counseling. She fought me at the beginning, but to this day, she thanks me for helping her to face her issues with a professional. "
—English Major, Washington University—St. Louis

" My roommate was depressed, and I told her about the university's counseling. She was surprised to find out that it was free. I went with her to her first appointment. "
—Economics Major, University of North Carolina—Chapel Hill

" My roommate was anorexic. I tried to be available and approachable, without being intrusive. Never be overly critical or forceful. Be a roommate and a friend and leave the actual 'treatment' to a trained professional. "
—Spanish Major, Yale University

" Sophomore year, one of my roommates was bulimic. My other roommates and I had an intervention and told her we were really worried about her. We agreed to go to a counselor with her and sit there the whole time. We used our student health services, and they were great. She is now doing a million times better. "
—**Classics Major, University of California—Santa Barbara**

Sexual Assault

The statistics about sexual assault you will read and hear when you first go away to college, unfortunately, are all too true. However, don't take the "that will never happen to me" approach to it—you really have to think about this reality of college life. Be smart about it. Here are some ideas for staying safe(r) during college:

★ **Establish a buddy system when you go to parties or other unknown situations.** Designate your buddy and never leave that person alone. You're there to watch out for each other.

★ **Find out how and where to contact campus security.** Some campuses have emergency call buttons or phones throughout campus. Learn where they are, or program campus security in your cell phone.

★ **Know your limits.** Alcohol can seriously impair your decision-making abilities and thus, lower your guard. Don't drink more than you can handle—or better yet, don't drink at all. College parties can be fun without being wasted.

And if anything does happen to you, be sure to take action. See the school nurse or health center, and contact campus security or the local police to report any incident so that you can hopefully prevent it from happening to someone else.

THE DOS AND DON'TS OF HELPING A ROOMMATE WHO HAS BEEN SEXUALLY ASSAULTED

If your roommate comes to you and tells you that she has been sexually assaulted or abused, the answer is not immediately to hunt down the slime who did it. Instead, take the following approach:

Do:

★ Tell your roommate it was not her fault. Most people blame themselves for what happened.

★ Let your roommate choose whether or not to report the assault. It is her choice. You should be supportive of her decision. However, you should advise your roommate that to keep that option open, she should keep all evidence. This means not showering or brushing teeth. The clothes she was wearing should be kept in a paper bag.

★ Encourage your roommate to get support and counseling.

Don't:

★ Hug or touch your roommate to offer support without asking first. Remember, she was just violated, and you don't want to retraumatize her.

★ Ask questions that begin with "Why?" You don't want to sound judgmental.

★ Judge. No matter what your roommate was drinking or wearing, it was NOT her fault.

★ Pressure. Let your roommate share only whatever details she is comfortable with.

Source: *http://spectrum.troy.edu/~save/html/howtohelp.html*

Alcohol Abuse

Most college students—especially freshmen—do not fully understand the effects of alcohol, and many wind up going too far. Here are some signs of alcohol abuse:

★ Missing classes and failing to complete assignments because of drinking

★ Noticeable changes in mood and behavior

★ Becoming angry and violent when drinking

★ Drinking alone

★ Drinking to escape problems or stressful situations

★ Continuing to drink even after previously getting in trouble due to alcohol consumption

THE DOS AND DON'TS OF HELPING A ROOMMATE WITH AN ALCOHOL ABUSE PROBLEM

If you recognize any of these signs in your roommate, you should try to get help:

Do:

★ Let your roommate know you are genuinely concerned and offer to go with him to student health services.

★ Be prepared to face resistance. If this happens, leave a telephone number to call for help on your roommate's desk or bed.

Don't:

★ Tell yourself it's just a phase your roommate is going through or that lots of college kids drink a lot. Ignoring it won't make it go away.

★ Beat around the bush when discussing your concern.

★ Believe that you alone can change your roommate's drinking habits.

Sources: *www.bc.edu/offices/bcpd/prevention/alcohol/* and *www.colby.edu/health.serv/drugs/friend.html*

Drug Abuse

There are many cases where one roommate has no problem with "social drug use" and the other roommate does. If your roommate is doing something illegal or something you are morally opposed to in your shared living space, stand your ground. You should never be made to feel uncomfortable in your own home. Speak up.

Remember, too, that there are no such things as legal drugs. You have to realize that many campuses have a zero tolerance for drug use. Consider whether that high is worth getting kicked out of school (or even going to jail) for! Drug use and abuse won't just be an issue for your RA, but you could find yourself face-to-face with the local police. Make the decisions that you know are right.

Just Say No

Illegal drug use and underage drinking should never be considered the norm when you go away to college. Here are ten thoughts from students who dealt with drinking and drug issues.

" I thought my roommate was drinking too much and neglecting her studies. Instead of saying anything, I began inviting her to study with me. I made studying a fun thing to do together, and this worked really well. "
—Political Science Major, Vanderbilt University

" My roommate and three other friends confronted my drinking problem by having an intervention. I had hit rock bottom. They saved my college career . . . they saved my life. "

—Public Relations Major, Mount Mercy College

" I found my roommate passed out on the floor of the bathroom with a black eye and chipped tooth. As scared as I was, when she sobered up, I think it scared her even more because she didn't know how she got there or how she got hurt. It never happened again. "

—English Major, New York University

" My roommate puked on my bed. I had to get the RA involved and that had a serious effect on my roommate's out-of-control drinking. "

—Anthropology Major, Emory University

" If you want to avoid party problems in your dorm room, declare the space alcohol-free from Day One. People can take the party elsewhere! "

—Art History Major, University of California—Davis

" My roommates would always smoke pot in our room. I'd ask them to stop, but they wouldn't. I complained that I was severely allergic to smoke (not true). After that, they tried to smoke outside the room. "

—Chemical Engineering Major, Cooper Union

" The most difficult conversation I ever had with my roommate was when I told her that she couldn't keep using illegal drugs in our house. She got really angry at me and acted like I was messing up her life—but she did take her drugs elsewhere. "

—Criminal Justice Major, University of Nevada—Las Vegas

" It was really hard to work out an agreement with my roommate to keep illegal drug use out of the common room in our house. He kept 'forgetting' about it, and I kept reminding him. It took a while, but it finally worked. "

—English Literature Major, University of Notre Dame

" One of my roommates was a serious drug user. To get her to stop, we had to threaten her with eviction. "

—Electrical Engineering Major, Texas A&M University

" When it comes to drugs, dropping subtle hints does not work—it really only pisses people off. You need to confront them head-on. "

—Telecommunications Major, Indiana University

READ THIS BOOK!

In *Smashed: Growing Up a Drunk Girl*, author Koren Zailckas immediately sets the tone for this unforgettable and brutally honest memoir. No detail is spared—from the first time drinking lands her in the hospital (during high school!) to the last time she wakes up in a total stranger's apartment (after college). But surprisingly, the book doesn't preach; instead, it includes staggering facts on binge drinking as well as some of the most seemingly unreal alcohol advertising around. By reading what she went through, hopefully, you won't have to go through it.

★ BE SMART; BE SAFE ★

It can be a mistake to assume that your life on campus will be like living in a utopia where crime is nonexistent. Thinking realistically, you know this is not true. While the most prevalent on-campus crimes are typically theft (no, you can't leave your iPod on the cafeteria table while you return your tray), other crimes such as sexual assault and breaking and entering can and do happen. However, this should not freak you out. Instead, it should prepare you to employ the same street smarts you have in the "outside" world to your life on campus. Use common sense to avoid things like walking through dark, secluded areas alone, inviting a total stranger back to your room, leaving a wad of cash lying around your unlocked dorm room, etc. Sound simple? It can be.

Keep reading to learn more about ways some students suggest staying safe on campus.

Safety First

Common sense is your first and best way to keep you and your belongings safe. However, here are ten thoughts from students who have other ideas about making sure that you and your stuff stay safe.

" A girl should know a guy before she lets him come to her house, and she should always meet him in a public setting for the first couple of dates. "
    —Journalism Major, University of Texas—Austin

" Never take an open drink from someone you don't know. "
    —Political Science Major, University of Massachusetts— Amherst

" Never walk home by yourself at night if you are intoxi-
cated; should something happen, you may not be in the
right frame of mind to handle it. Don't let people who
have been drinking drive you anywhere—just call the
campus shuttle or a cab! "
     —**Biology Major, Oberlin College**

" Be aware of the people around you at all times. Most
campuses have police who will escort you on campus.
Use this service if you feel the slightest concern for your
safety. Get a cell phone and know their number and the
number for roadside assistance. "
     —**English Major, Texas Women's University**

" Never put yourself in a situation where no one knows
where you are. If you didn't come home, how long would
it be before anyone noticed? "
     —**Psychology Major, University of Alabama**

" Although you should be open to new ideas and people,
your room shouldn't. Always lock it when you're not
there. "
     —**Legal Studies Major, Quinnipiac University**

" Don't leave your stuff lying around. As much as you'd like to believe that no one wants your biochemistry book, you'd be surprised—there are weirdos out there. "
—**Psychology Major, University of Michigan—Ann Arbor**

" Keep your stuff with you when you are in the library; so many people get their bags stolen. "
—**Biology Major, Oberlin College**

" Don't bring too much expensive stuff to college. Make sure that everything you really care about is kept in a secure place and that the rest can be replaced easily. "
—**Political Science Major, University of California—San Diego**

" Visit campus security to see what advice they have. For example, our security office has this software program that can track your laptop if it gets stolen. "
—**Biochemistry/Spanish Major, University of Wisconsin— Madison**

Just because you know that bad things can happen in college doesn't mean that you are now immune to problems like these. Learn from others' mistakes and make sure that your college years are as safe and fun as they can be.

Speaking of fun—let's move on to other college essentials—hookups, breakups, and other activities!

Hookups, Breakups, and Other College Activities

If you're anything like me, you might have skipped the first five chapters of this book and gone straight for the juicy stuff. I mean, who doesn't want to know more about all the thrills that college holds in store?! And yes, there is no shortage of hookup opportunities in college. But it's not all just about that.

On the flipside, maybe going away to college means leaving behind your high school sweetheart. Or once you do get your first significant other in college, you are broken up before you even go home for Thanksgiving. College provides for all of these opportunities—the good hookups, the bad love hangovers, and the ugly breakups. ★

But college is not just about how much action you see . . . there are plenty of other college activities you should be aware of. From intramural sports (Ultimate Frisbee!) to volunteerism, you will undoubtedly find something you like to do with your spare time. And if you feel like you can't spend another minute on campus, there is always studying abroad!

This chapter is your one-stop shop for information and advice on all of these topics. Remember, current students and recent grads have seen and done it all. Learn what you can, but never forget that whatever you do, have fun doing it!

★ HOOKUPS! ★

You and the hottie from down the hall are entwined in a down-and-dirty lip lock. Suddenly, the door bangs open and in barges your roommate. As he clicks on the computer to check IMs, the steam from your kisses turns cold. Welcome to dorm room lovin'!

With two or more people sharing a small space in a hormonally charged dorm, romance is sure to fire up problems unless rules and boundaries are set right away. In this part of the chapter, we'll weigh in on the rules of hooking up, what to do when both roommates need the room for love, and how to signal to your roommate that the room is otherwise "occupied" without being rude.

Get Some (Advice, That Is)

As great as college hookups can be, there are still some things you need to be aware of. Here are ten thoughts on hooking up from experienced students and recent grads.

" Word travels fast around campus, so don't do anything you don't want to hear about from your neighbor's lab partner's best friend the next day! "
    —Psychology Major, Muhlenberg College

" Drunken hookups are a part of college, so relish the walk of shame! "
— **Economics Major, Cornell University**

" Generally, it helps to know the person's name before you hook up with them. Chances are, you're going to run into them again. "
— **Biological Sciences Major, Rutgers University**

" Don't kiss and tell. If you do, people won't just start talking about the person you kissed—they'll start talking about you, too. "
— **Chemical Engineering Major, University of Rhode Island**

" If you're going to have a guest spend the night in your room, make sure to inform your roommate. Many an awkward situation has occurred when people don't follow this rule. "
— **Communications Major, Cornell University**

" It isn't the best idea to hook up with someone in one of your classes. Because if it doesn't work out, it can get awkward when you have to sit next to them for 55 minutes three times a week. "
— **Chemistry Major, University of Chicago**

" Don't confuse hooking up with dating. It's easy to get your feelings hurt in college when one person thinks they're in a relationship and the other just thinks he or she is having a good time. "
—**English Major, Princeton University**

" Forget about any long-distance relationship you started in high school. It sounds harsh, but chances are, it's not going to last. "
—**Writing Major, Emerson College**

" Having a boyfriend/girlfriend is great, but don't get involved with a slacker who will keep you from studying. "
—**Pharmacology Major, University of Connecticut**

" It's exciting to have a boyfriend or girlfriend at college because you can spend all your time with that person. But don't! There are new friends to make, clubs to join, and opportunities to explore. Don't get so wrapped up in your relationship that you miss it all. "
—**Art Major, University of Hawaii—Manoa**

★ THREE'S A CROWD ★

Maybe your boyfriend wants to spend every minute with you. Maybe you want to be with your girlfriend all the time. Sounds like the perfect plan—if you lived alone! Students warn that having your boyfriend or girlfriend in your room 24/7 is bound to create major roommate tension. The living space is small, and even if your roommate gets along really well with your significant other, hanging out with the two of you day in and day out is not what she signed on for. Here are some tips to keep you and your roommate happy:

★ **Don't step over the line.** Make sure your significant other knows the boundaries. He may be close with you, but this is not his room. The fridge is not a free-for-all. It is not okay for him to lounge on your roommate's bed.

★ **Be proactive.** If your significant other is becoming a nuisance to your roommate, you are the one who needs to talk to your romantic interest—not your roommate.

★ **Alternate.** Share the love and don't overextend your roommate's hospitality. Alternate between your significant other's place and yours.

★ **Keep PDAs to a minimum.** Do you want to witness your roommate's girlfriend groping him? Not a chance! Well, it goes the same way for your roommate, too. Keep your hands to yourselves when the two of you are not alone.

What happens if you're the one who's flying solo for the moment, but your roommate has a boyfriend or girlfriend who's always around? Here are some ideas for peace, love, and understanding:

★ **Play nice.** Your roommate likes this guy, so we're sure she'd appreciate it if you try to be nice to him (even if you can't for the life of you figure out why she'd want to date such a loser).

★ **Have a private conversation.** If your roommate's girlfriend is annoying you to no end or has turned your desk into her own private vanity, confront your roommate, but do it without his girlfriend present. (Make an appointment with him to talk alone if you have to.) Try to have a clear and rational conversation. Do not criticize his girlfriend or accuse him of being "whipped"—instead offer some solutions to the problem.

★ **Knock first.** If you think there's a good chance your roommate's significant other is there, knock before barging in. True, you have a right to enter your own room, but you should also respect your roommate's privacy. (Plus it might save you from seeing something you just don't want to see!)

★ **Discourage PDAs.** If your roommate's displays of affection are more than you are comfortable witnessing up close and personal, tell her. It is okay to make rules like, "No hooking up in the room if the other roommate is there." Remember, it is your home too, and you get an equal say as to what can or cannot happen.

★ **Avoid the third-wheel syndrome.** Your roommate used to go to the dining hall every night with you for dinner, and now he brings his girlfriend too. Your roommate used to listen to the daily saga of your crush on that hot senior, but now her boyfriend is always adding his (unhelpful) opinions. Don't let yourself be dragged down because your roommate has a significant other. Search out the unattached in your dorm—they are sure to be a lot more fun than your roommate is these days!

Setting Up to Get Down

There should always be some kind of ground rules for hooking up, especially when a roommate is involved. Here are ten thoughts from students on the best way to deal when three's company.

" A significant other could spend the night if we asked first, and the other roommate would spend the night at a friend's. But we agreed that at exam or finals time, visitors were not allowed. "
   —Biochemistry/Molecular Biology Major, Boston College

" If my boyfriend and I wanted some alone time and my roommate was around, we'd always leave the room and find someplace else on campus to go. Who wants to be in a loud, unromantic dorm room with your love interest anyway? "
   —Public Relations Major, University of Georgia

" I would often wake up in the middle of the night to hear my roommate and her boyfriend making out above me in the top bunk when they thought I was asleep. Not OK! To avoid having to crawl out of your room commando style because you are too embarrassed to say something at that moment, talk about what to do ahead of time— before it becomes an issue. "
   —Legal Studies Major, University of Massachusetts—Amherst

" When my roommate's boyfriend visited, I left the room, and I always gave her an approximate time when I would return. "
   —History Major, University of Colorado—Boulder

" We would tell the other to leave the room. This was one of the advantages of being roommates with someone who is your friend. "
—**Nutrition Major, State University of New York—Stony Brook**

" With random hookups, both roommates often feel that their privacy is compromised. The one hooking up feels he or she deserves a little privacy to boogie down in the room, and the other roommate feels he or she deserves to be able to enter his or her own room when he or she wants to. You've got to talk this out, so there's equal give-and-take from both of you. "
—**Government Major, Georgetown University**

" I wish I had told my roommate that I minded when her boyfriend slept over instead of trying to avoid a fight. As a result, I think he spent more time in my room than I did! "
—**Business Administration Major, University of Delaware**

" When my roommate wanted to take 'naps' with his girlfriend, I would take an extended shower and a leisurely shave. "
—**Program II Major, Duke University**

" We would try to disappear as much as possible to leave the other one alone if one of our boyfriends was over. "
—**International Relations Major, San Francisco State University**

" My freshman year roommate's boyfriend was forever coming over to make out with her after I fell asleep. The trouble is that with just a few feet between beds, even the heaviest sleeper is going to wake up with that kind of thing going on. My roommate would die if I ever told her what I saw! "
—**History Major, Duke University**

THE "BOOTY CALL" COMMANDMENTS

Have you ever been in the situation where you come home to repeatedly find your roommate rolling around with some guy or girl that you've never seen before? There are special roommate rules for this kind of casual situation. Whether it's you or your roommate who's doing the hooking up, be mindful of the following commandments:

★ Thou shalt not take your roommate's condoms and leave him stuck for Saturday night.

★ Thou shalt not leave any evidence of a romantic encounter.

★ Thou shalt not get hot and heavy with someone five minutes before your roommate is due home.

★ Thou shalt not have an all-night lovefest while your roommate is cooling her heels in the lounge.

★ Thou shalt not have relations on your roommate's bed, desk, towels, or side of the room.

★ Thou shalt not hook up while your roommate is in the room—awake or asleep.

"Do Not Disturb" Code Words and Other Hookup Advice

Turning your dorm room into a temporary love nest is possible but not always advisable. Here are ten thoughts from students about how to make sure everyone gets a little satisfaction.

" We didn't bother with code words. Instead, we promised to never 'sexile' each other (kick your roommate out of the room for the purposes of hooking up). If that meant waiting until the other one was out of the room, then so be it! "
        —Political Science Major, New York University

" Never assume your roommate is asleep! "
        —Legal Studies Major, University of Massachusetts—Amherst

" Don't forget that the person you are hooking up with has a place to live, too. You need to compromise and have one roommate go elsewhere. "
—**Anthropology Major, University of Western Ontario**

" If my roommate and I both needed the room, we would rock-paper-scissors for it. "
—**Pre-Medicine Major, St. Mary's College**

" We placed a code word on the dry-erase board hanging outside our door. BONZAI!!! was the signal to find some-place else to sleep. "
—**Political Science Major, Pennsylvania State University**

" We developed a system where the privacy-seeking roommate would lock the door and put a piece of clear tape over the lock, so if the other roommate came home to discover the door locked and taped, she would know not to come a-knockin'. "
—**Economics Major, Bucknell University**

" We placed a hairband on the handle outside if we wanted to be alone. "
—**Political Science Major, Shippensburg University**

" 'We need milk' was the code word for the dry-erase board. "
—**Food Science Major, Alma College**

" We had a knock pattern. That helped us warn each other before interrupting something personal. "
—**Finance/Communication Major, University of South Florida**

" We worked out a signal on the door: we had a little paper heart laminated, and we would stick it on the door if we brought someone back with us. The other person would then knock twice and say she'd be back in a few minutes. "
—**Psychology Major, University of Illinois—Urbana-Champaign**

★ BREAKING UP IS HARD TO DO ★

You come home from class, and your roommate is trying to punch through the cinder block wall or is in tears, rocking back and forth in the fetal position. You don't have to be a detective to know that your roomie was dumped. Now you are left to pick up the pieces of your roommate's pulverized heart. Here are some tips to help the healing process:

★ **Listen.** Even if that means enduring the 85th retelling of the story of how they were meant to be together and hearing the same sappy CD of "their song" over and over.

★ **Sympathize.** A broken heart hurts immensely. This is not the time for "I told you so."

★ **Go fishing.** Okay, not literally. But when the wallowing in grief has run its course, motivate your roommate to forget about his sorrows. Show him that there are "plenty of fish in the sea" and head with him to a party, a bar, or a club meeting.

★ **Bite your tongue.** It's fun for your roommate to trash her ex—and it does make her feel better!— but before you join in the bashing, think about this: there's a very good chance that your roommate and the guy she hates today will kiss and make up tomorrow . . . and that she'll always remember you bad-mouthing her sweetie.

Surviving the Breakup

Everyone gets their heart broken at some point. Here are ten thoughts from students about facing a new day following a bad break up.

" If it's an especially bad breakup, be sure to take the time you really need to recover. Don't just impulsively fall into heavy partying or ignoring your school work. You don't want the breakup to negatively affect everything else in your life. "
—Art History Major, University of California—Davis

" The best thing my roommate ever did was kick her boyfriend out of our room when I came home one night after I had broken up with my boyfriend. She let me talk and cry. It was just what I needed. "
—Political Science Major, Barnard College

" One of my roommates went through a period of depression and self-destructive behavior after she broke up with her long-term boyfriend. All the other roommates agreed to never let her be by herself. We tried to keep her entertained to keep her mind off things. "
—English Major, University of California—Santa Barbara

" Always agree that [the ex] was clearly out of his or her mind. "
—Journalism Major, University of South Carolina

" Even if you're not that close with your roommate, for girls, hugs are key. "
—**International Affairs Major, George Washington University**

" For girls, Ben & Jerry's cures all! "
—**Psychology Major, Georgetown University**

" If your roommate is a guy, just distract him with a party full of girls. "
—**History Major, Columbia University**

" I passed an ex-boyfriend to my roommate, and she ended up marrying him! "
—**Sociology Major, Pennsylvania State University**

" Revenge is not the answer—finding someone new is! "
—**Anthropology Major, Emory University**

" When my roommate got dumped, it only inspired him to be a better boyfriend and to try to win her back. Dinner, flowers, and a Hallmark card worked—they got back together and stayed that way for a long time! "
—**English Major, Tufts University**

★ EXTRACURRICULAR ACTIVITIES ★

Believe it or not, you're likely to be too busy to find yourself watching a *Real World* marathon on TV. After all, college campuses are packed with 17- to 22-year olds, so there is no shortage of things to do. The thing to do is to find something you like and commit. Trying out different activities once or twice is fine, but being a flake won't improve your life outside of class. Here are just a few options you will have on campus: clubs, volunteerism, and sports.

Clubs

You would have to be completely disinterested or unbelievably unique to not find any club or organization to join. Think you're the only Weird Al fan on campus? Think you won't find other people who speak Lithuanian? Think you are the only lesbian enrolled at your school? Think again! The diversity of most college campuses ensures that if you can think of it, there is probably a club or organization already formed. Visit your school's Web site or check out the student activities office when you arrive to find out exactly what is available to you. And don't forget—if there is no club or organization for your interests, why not start one? You never know how many other students on campus are interested in the same things you are!

Volunteer Activities

I know it sounds cliché, but volunteering really does as much good for you as it does for those you are trying to help. Whether you volunteer on campus for a student support help line or you help build houses with Habitat for Humanity, it will be a rewarding experience. Volunteering can also be something you already love doing. Do you love playing piano? Consider giving a concert at the local senior citizen center. Do you love getting off campus and driving around your new city? Think about volunteering for Meals on Wheels. If your school has a volunteer center on campus, start your search there. If not, go online and search for volunteer opportunities in the local community. You won't regret it!

Sports

Yes, there is no shortage of students who go to school on athletic scholarships. However, you don't have to be a Division I tennis player to find some physical challenges at college. First, if your school has a gym, see what kinds of programs or classes are offered. If organized sports are more your thing, check out what kind of intramural (recreational) sports are offered at your school. There are perennial favorites such as Ultimate Frisbee, but also look out for less common sports such as speed skating or cricket. And the best thing about intramural sports is that they are usually offered at different levels. So even if you've never picked up a lacrosse stick, you can still join a team for a little friendly competition. Of course, if you are able to play at the varsity level, you will have the added experience of playing against other schools and getting amazing experience playing collegiate sports.

Getting Involved

So now you know that college isn't just about academics and romance. Here are ten thoughts from students on how to make the most of the extracurricular opportunities you will have in college.

" Extracurriculars get you away from the television and add structure and balance to your life. "
    —**Business Administration Major, Morehouse College**

" I suggest going to as many different meetings as possible. Even if you're only remotely interested in the club, it might present something that will convince you it's worth your time. "
    —**Sociology Major, University of California—Irvine**

" You will never again have the opportunity to do so many varied things or have access to the kinds of resources that a university offers. Take advantage of them while you can. "
    —**Biology/Pre-Medicine Major, Oklahoma Christian University**

" Extracurricular activities are like a buffet: try a little bit of this and a little bit of that. Don't join anything right away—give each option some time so that you can decide what interests you enough to pursue further. "
— **Political Science Major, University of Notre Dame**

" It's good to pursue leadership roles and participate in community service because it'll look excellent on your résumé or applications for professional schools—and it's fun and a great way to meet new people who share the same interests as you. "
— **Psychology Major, University of Alabama—Huntsville**

" Playing intramural sports is great because you do just as much socializing as you do practicing—it's much more low-key than a varsity sport, but you still have a great time and get exercise. "
— **Mathematical Economics Major, Colgate University**

" I always loved sports, but I didn't have the time (or talent) to play for a Division I team. Instead, I joined a bunch of intramural leagues that were a blast and also a great way to meet people who shared my interests. "
— **Legal Studies Major, Quinnipiac University**

" I have been a mentor for inner-city African American males and a member of Noon Run, an organization that makes and serves lunches to the homeless. I wanted to take advantage of the diverse culture that Milwaukee offers and interact with people that I normally would never meet. "
— **Biomedical Sciences Major, Marquette University**

" Find an activity you're interested in and go participate in it. It doesn't matter if it's academic, athletic, or something else. If the activity interests you, you'll likely find people who interest you there. "
— **Informatics Major, University of Washington**

" Attend events that support issues that you are adamant about—it's the best way to find people who share the same interests as you. "
— **Political Economy of Industrial Societies, University of California—Berkeley**

THINKING AHEAD

Although it shouldn't be the only reason you get involved in extracurricular activities, having something to put on your résumé after graduation doesn't hurt. Anyone can go to college and get good grades, but it takes an especially motivated and responsible student to balance academics and other activities. Leadership positions are even better. They show your commitment and your ability to lead and manage others. Make the most of your free time, and you will have something to show for it when you are ready to enter the "real world."

★ STUDY ABROAD ★

You probably know that sometimes a change in scenery is just what the doctor ordered. I mean, you've spent months and countless hours inside the bubble that is your campus, and there will come a time when you'll want to break free and try something new. That's why study abroad is such a great option. You can meet new people (locals are best!) and possibly even learn a new language.

There are typically three options for studying abroad. You can study for a semester, a year, or a summer. There are pros and cons to each, so consider these questions before you make your decision:

★ Will the study abroad program interfere with my regular major and graduation requirements? If so, perhaps a summer program is best for you.

★ Am I going to learn a new language and fully immerse myself in a different culture? A semester is fine, but a year in a different country is ideal.

★ Do I want to maintain my studies at my current school but still get some exposure in a different country? A semester abroad is probably the way to go.

Of course, there will be plenty of other things to keep in mind when studying abroad. Visas, housing, and coursework are all considerations. Make an appointment at your school's study abroad office to learn about the programs offered by your school or programs that are offered by other schools but accepted by yours. You can also do some research online. Student travel blogs are everywhere. You might read something that will inspire you!

BRANCH OUT!

When you are studying or traveling abroad, it's easy to stick close to students in the program you already know. However, if you're just there to hang out with students from your own university, why are you studying abroad in the first place? Although it might be intimidating to meet locals, especially if there's a major language barrier, it's these types of experiences that make study abroad so unique. Plus, a local's knowledge of nontouristy places will surely provide you with some memorable experiences with landscape, food, music, and culture.

Frequent Flyers

Even if you speak a foreign language fluently, it's always a good idea to have some advice from other travelers. Here are ten thoughts from students about traveling abroad.

" A good guidebook does wonders."
    —Sociology Major, Colgate College

" I traveled to Russia to work in orphanages with some people from my department; it changed my life. I would suggest that everyone travel abroad if they can."
    —Speech Pathology Major, Towson University

" My most memorable experience was the summer I spent abroad. I worked for two months, first in London, completely on my own, and then I studied through a school program at Oxford University. The entire experience was absolutely invaluable; I matured and grew in more ways than I could possibly have foreseen. And a big part of that was just getting far away from everyone and everything that was familiar to me."
    —Psychology Major, University of Texas—Austin

" If you spend a semester on another continent like Europe, make sure you travel to as many countries as possible during your time there. When will you get another chance to have a home base so close to so many new experiences? "
    —**English Major, Princeton University**

" The thought of moving to another continent might sound scary, but this is the only time in your life when you'll be able to just pick up and go. Don't waste the opportunity. "
    —**Government Major, Connecticut College**

" Go to a place where you are fluent in the language so that you can fully immerse yourself in the culture. "
    —**Biology Major, Emory University**

" If you're worried about the cost of going abroad, there are special loans for this kind of thing. Check with your abroad office to see what your school offers. "
    —**Mechanical Engineering Major, University of Evansville**

" Be sure you at least know how to say thank you when you travel abroad in a country where you don't speak the language. It came in very handy the first few days, especially, and throughout the entire semester. Oh, and it helps to know the word for beer too! "
    —Computer Science Major, Union College

" Do your best to learn about the culture and etiquette of a country before you go. For example, I studied in Italy where, despite the popularity of wine, it's frowned upon to get really drunk. It was easy to spot the American students around town because they were the only ones completely wasted at the bars and clubs. It really doesn't do much for the image of Americans around the world. "
    —Spanish Major, New York University

" When I decided to spend my entire junior year abroad, I was panicked that no one would remember me when I came back and that I would have a hard time organizing student housing and roommates. It turns out I shouldn't have worried about any of that. Lots of people studied abroad that year and it was actually great being welcomed back my senior year. I'm glad I didn't let my fears affect my decision. Wunderbar! (That's 'wonderful' in German!) "
    —German Major, Emory University

Aaah . . . the joys and sorrows of hooking up and breaking up and everything else college has to offer may leave you wondering . . . what about one of the ultimate college activities—Greek life? Keep reading and you'll learn everything you wanted to know about joining a fraternity or sorority on campus.

Going Greek?

I'll admit it. I was so COMPLETELY clueless about the Greek system, fraternities, and sororities when I went to college, it was embarrassing. Actually, all I really knew about the entire system I had learned from party/teen movies. Obviously, Hollywood is not a particularly accurate or reliable source of information, so when I finally got on campus, I had to learn what I could from experience. The truth was, I still didn't really know what was going on and what all the terminology meant—and I was definitely too afraid to ask—I mean, I was at a southern school which prided itself on being more than 50 percent Greek!

Nevertheless, second semester of my freshman year, I participated in rush, accepted a bid, and even pledged a sorority. It all happened so fast that when I had the time to sit and think about what I was doing and how much I was paying (more on that later), I realized that it wasn't really what I wanted, and as a result, I never reached the initiation process. ★

WARNING: I'm about to state the obvious. An informed decision is really the best one to make, so that's why this chapter presents you with plenty of information about the basics on Greek life. Keep in mind that this is generalized and might not be specific to your school. Take the advice in this chapter or not, as you wish. Remember, as fraternity or sorority members, people who are quoted here are sharing opinions that are definitely subjective. Take into account what they are saying, but don't forget to think and decide for yourself about what is best for you.

Let's get started with a glossary of terms.

★ GREEK LIFE GLOSSARY ★

It's easy to sound like a seasoned student when you are able to wax philosophically on subjects like rush, bids, and pledging. However, don't worry if you don't know exactly what these and other terms mean. Read this section carefully, so that you know what people are really talking about. The terms are listed in the general order in which they occur during entrance to a Greek organization.

Greek system/Greek life

This is the generic term for fraternities and sororities found across the United States. Fraternities and sororities are named after letters of the Greek alphabet, for example, Sigma Chi or Kappa Kappa Gamma. That's why this is commonly referred to as the Greek system or Greek life—it has nothing to do with your ancestry!

Fraternity

Although fraternities are typically thought of as all-male organizations, there are actually co-ed fraternities as well. As an organization, a fraternity establishes and maintains certain personal and public ideals. Fraternities are national, but each school has its own chapter. In addition to typical social fraternities (which tend to be all-male), there are service, professional, and honorary fraternities.

Brother

In typical social fraternities, this is what members are called. Like a family, there are big brothers (upperclassmen) and little brothers (new members). In turn, little brothers will become big brothers as a new group of pledges arrives. The more generic term *active* refers to any active member of a fraternity.

Sorority

Sororities are all-female organizations. As an organization, a sorority establishes and maintains certain personal and public ideals. Sororities are national, but each school has its own chapter.

Sister

In sororities, this is what members are called. Like a family, there are big sisters (upperclassmen) and little sisters (new members). In turn, little sisters will become big sisters as a new group of pledges arrives. The more generic term *active* refers to any active member of a sorority.

Chapter

This is a smaller part of a national fraternity or sorority; each school has its own chapter.

House

A common misconception is that every fraternity or sorority has a sprawling house where wild parties are held every weekend. In truth, the house is synonymous with the chapter. It doesn't actually refer to the building itself, although in many cases it does.

Rush

Rush is when anyone who wants to join a fraternity or sorority visits the houses. It is a recruitment process that has several guidelines that must be followed by the chapter and by the rushees. (You can find more about rush later in this chapter.)

Bid

Following rush is bid day. This is when fraternities and sororities extend an invitation to join their chapter of the organization.

Pledge

Once a student accepts a bid from a fraternity or sorority, this person is referred to as a pledge. That person has pledged to join the organization.

Initiation

Following a specific pledge period and just after initiation week, pledges participate in initiation. The process of initiation is meant to be top secret. You won't know anything about it before you go through it, and you are not allowed to share any of the rituals that take place during initiation. After you have completed initiation, you are a full-fledged member of that fraternity and sorority.

There are two more terms you might want to familiarize yourself with, although they are not standard elements to Greek life.

Hazing

This word seems to have nothing but negative press. When you hear "hazing," you might be thinking about pledges forced to drink until they die of alcohol poisoning or being beaten with a paddle until unconscious. Unfortunately, these incidents have happened. However, there are many more completely harmless activities that may be expected of you as a pledge or new member. This may include wearing a ridiculous outfit to class or cleaning a brother's or sister's apartment. If you do find these kinds of activities too degrading, you can rely on antihazing policies that are in place with nearly every organization. You should never be forced to do something you don't want to do. Think about it. Would you really want to be part of something that is keen to put you through emotional or physical torture?

GDI

G** D*** Independent. Making a play on the three letters of many organization names, this is reserved for those who choose not to join a fraternity or sorority.

YES, YOU WILL BE TESTED ON THIS

As a pledge, you are expected to learn as much as you can about the history and traditions of your fraternity or sorority. You're not just there for bonding and parties; you are there to uphold the traditions of your organization. You can and should expect quizzes and drills on everything from the founders of the organization to current statistics about the organization at your school.

Glad to Be Greek

Here are ten thoughts from students who joined the Greek system while in school.

" I am involved in a national service fraternity, which is not only personally fulfilling but also benefits others. "
—**Biomedical Engineering Major, Saint Louis University**

" I pledged a sorority, and it was the best thing I did throughout my college career. It opened so many doors and introduced me to my very best friends. I would recommend it to anyone. "
—**Communications Major, Northeastern State University**

" In actuality I never imagined joining a fraternity, but once I met the other guys there, we all clicked, and it made sense to join since I hung out with them a great deal anyway. "
—**Russian Major, Johns Hopkins University**

" My most memorable experiences involved just hanging out in my fraternity house with all my friends. Spring break in Amsterdam with nine of my fraternity brothers was one of the greatest times of my life. "
—**Philosophy Major, State University of New York—Binghamton**

" I was in a business fraternity. I joined at first for networking, but I have also made so many new friends and participated in so many activities. "
—**Business Administration Major, University of Missouri—Columbia**

" I was in a sorority because it was a good way to get involved, both socially and within the community. Also, networking with alumni to find a job was important! "
—**Anthropology Major, Northwestern University**

" I am in a sorority because I love that I feel like I'm at camp when I'm really at school! "
—**Psychology Major, University of Michigan**

" Fraternities and sororities are also good sources for getting old exams to study from for your classes. "
—**History Major, Colgate University**

" My biggest regret was not joining my sorority sooner. Those girls were my closest friends, and they made my schoolwork so much easier to do. College life as a whole was better just because they were there. "
—**Environmental Studies Major, Emory & Henry College**

" Sorority life completely changed my experience on campus. As cheesy as it sounds, I really felt like I was part of a big family. "

—English Major, Emory University

WORTH THE WAIT

Every school has it's own rules about when rush can occur. At some schools, you have to wait until second semester of freshman year, while other schools require students to wait until their sophomore year. While this may seem restrictive, imagine if rush began on the first day of school. Your first interactions would be only with other fraternities and sororities, and you wouldn't really have the chance to find your own niche. Remember, you don't have to rush right away. Taking some time to interact and settle in could make a big difference in your college experience.

But don't take my word for it. Here is what one student had to say about waiting.

" For some people it's better to wait until sophomore year than to rush a fraternity or sorority as a freshman. How can you possibly say, 'I want to be a member of this organization for four years,' based on one week of interaction with the members? "

—Economics Major, DePauw University

★ HURRY UP AND RUSH! ★

You read about rush in the Greek Life Glossary—now it's time to learn more about this important first step into the Greek system. As you now know, rush is when anyone who wants to join a fraternity or sorority visits the houses. However, this is not a casual "I just happened to be in the neighborhood" visit. Rush, which can last as long as one week, is a structured recruitment process.

Rush varies from school to school, but the general idea is that you meet with all of the houses to find out which one suits you best and which one current members think YOU suit best. For example, on the first day, you typically meet every house. After that, each house makes a decision on whether it wants to meet you again. This goes on until the last day, when bids are offered (or not). You have to accept the fact that you are not going to be asked back to every house. In many cases, this is a blessing, because you will know right away that some houses really don't suit your style. Of course, if you decide that, in general, Greek life is not for you, you are certainly able to remove yourself from rush completely. There's always next year's rush!

Top Five Rush Tips

Here are five tips to keep your sanity during rush:

1. **Be yourself.** Members meet enough people during rush to know who's being real and who's putting on a show. Being fake (fake nice, fake interested, fake knowledgeable) is not going to get you an invitation to visit again. Do your best to calm your nerves and be exactly who you are, not who you think they want you to be.

2. **Be polite.** Even if you have no interest in returning to a particular organization, acting bored or pretending you are too good for a certain house is a big no-no. Although bid decisions are made independently, word is sure to spread to other houses if you are copping an attitude.

3. **Dress appropriately.** Many houses will give you clear directions on appropriate dress. Rush is not the time to show off the toga you had made for wild parties. It can be just the opposite, requiring you to wear more formal and dressy clothes than you would normally wear as a college student. Don't worry about impressing others with designer labels. As long as your outfit is clean, wrinkle-free, and fits you well, you are fine.

4. **Use your common sense.** You're not there to brag, show off, talk trash, or party. You are there to meet current members and decide where you think you will fit in. Don't do anything that could negatively affect your chances of being invited back or receiving a bid.

5. **Trust your gut.** From a fraternity's or sorority's perspective, rush is a way to market their organization as best as possible. If you think what you are hearing is too good to be true, chances are, it probably is. Learn to hear what they are saying, but also to listen to your intuition. The same rule applies when it comes time to accept a bid or not. You are the best judge of whether you will really fit in a certain house.

Your Turn to Ask Questions

Remember that when you are at a rush meeting, you are there to meet other members and to learn as much as you can about the organization. Here are some questions you should ask:

★ What is your favorite thing about this organization?

★ What causes does this organization support?

★ What is your favorite fraternity/sorority activity?

★ How long is the pledge process?

★ How much time are pledges required to dedicate to the organization?

★ When is the initiation?

★ Are there academic requirements for this organization? (Some chapters have minimum GPAs for students to remain active.)

★ Are any scholarships or grants offered by the organization?

★ During the pledge period, are all events mandatory?

Of course, to get to know the active members, don't forget to ask more general questions such as:

★ Where are you from?

★ What is your major?

★ What do you like to do with your free time?

★ What dorm do you live in, or do you live in the house?

★ What year are you?

★ What's your favorite book/movie/food/etc.?

Avoid Asking These Questions

These questions and topics are best avoided during rush:

★ **What are the secret rituals or handshakes?** This information is only for active members.

★ **How much alcohol do you drink?** Sure, you want to know whether this organization can party, but discussions about alcohol are completely inappropriate—and most likely forbidden by the organization.

★ **What is initiation like?** Remember, this is kept secret!

★ **How much does it cost?** This is not the time to seek out this information. Wait until you actually have a bid before you worry about costs.

THERE ARE NO GUARANTEES

Unless your school has a rule about offering bids to every rushee, rushing a fraternity or sorority unfortunately does not guarantee you a bid. In truth, just wanting it badly enough does not mean there is a place for you. Take it in stride if you are not offered a bid. There is always next year, or it may be a wake-up call to the reality that Greek life is not for you. Here is how one student handled it when her friend didn't make the cut.

" My roommate was cut from every sorority during rush. Almost everyone on our hall had pledged, and she felt very left out and very rejected. I tried to be around a lot and not make a big deal out of my sorority functions. I also tried to casually include her in activities with my new Greek friends. "

—**History Major, Wake Forest University**

★ IT'S GOING TO COST YOU! ★

So you want to go Greek? It can be tons of fun, but like any extracurricular activity, it's going to cost you money to join. Don't be surprised to find out that you'll start spending before you're even a full-fledged member. In fact, the first year is the most expensive. Initiation fees for pledges can cost several hundred dollars.

Check out these additional things you might be expected to dole out money for before you become a member:

★ **Clothing for pledging.** It may be neon or in other ways embarrassing, but expect a uniform of sorts to make it obvious you're a pledge.

★ **Group activities.** Whether it's dinner or a road trip, part of pledging means joining in when they tell you to, so be prepared for whatever cost comes along with these activities.

★ **Supplies.** You might be called on to make posters for members of your fraternity or sorority or to design a decorative piñata for a theme party. Try to get creative with your resources so you can save money. Look around your room or even in your classrooms (no "borrowing"!) for things you can use.

PAYING YOUR DUES

Here are a couple of points you need to keep in mind when you have decided whether or not to pledge:

★ Greek life is social life. In addition to your dues, you will be paying for formals, materials for community service projects, and more.

★ If you live outside the house, you'll not only have to pay for your own housing costs, but you'll also be paying for the upkeep of the fraternity or sorority house.

I Have to Pay for That?!?

When you are caught up in the excitement of receiving a bid and deciding to pledge, it's very easy to overlook some of the "hidden" costs of the Greek system. Keep in mind that not all of these costs are required by every organization, but you should be aware of them when you are budgeting for your new life as a sister or brother.

★ **Parties/formals.** This is why you joined Greek life. This is what's going to cost you the most. You have to fund these events and also rent tuxes, buy dresses, and make costumes. Exchange outfits and accessories with your brothers and sisters to keep costs down.

★ **Charity events.** All fraternities and sororities perform some sort of community service. Whether it's
fundraising for the local animal shelter or cleaning
up a community park, expect to spend time and
money on charity. If your budget's tight, volunteer
your time instead of your money.

★ **Sharing food with a house full of people.**
Don't be surprised if your bulk pack of 20 bagels is
missing the day after you buy it. Most of the food
in the house will be provided for you—try to make
do with what's available, and you'll save money. Or
you could always hide extra food in your room!

★ **Commemorative photos.** Many colleges have a
system where someone comes and takes pictures
at parties and events and then you can look
through the proofs and buy them. Ask yourself
before buying, "Do I really need this picture with
the same people I've already taken 65 other pictures with?" It will save you money to just bring
your own camera or purchase a disposable
camera and capture your own memories.

★ **Fees for not attending an event.** The rules
differ for every fraternity or sorority, but if you
miss an event or fail to perform certain duties, you
are often charged for your slipup.

★ CAN'T AFFORD IT! ★

It's an undisputable reality—being part of a fraternity or sorority can be very expensive. In fact, many students simply cannot be part of the Greek systems as a result of this. If you find yourself in this situation, you are not alone. Here are ten thoughts from students who had difficulty justifying the cost of joining Greek life.

" I cannot afford the $800 to get into the sorority I want to be in. I would also have to pay an additional $200 per year. That is unrealistic to me. "
—Communication Major, University of Pennsylvania

" I was a member for about two weeks, but I was always broke due to their fees so I just decided to skip that whole experience. I'm better off now than I was then. I have more privacy and more money to my name at the end of the day. "
—Pre-Medicine Major, El Paso Community College

" By the time you're a senior, you end up hanging out at places that don't involve your fraternity or sorority. Also, at most Greek events, the members can invite whomever they want. You don't have to be a member of that sorority or fraternity to attend the fun parties. Decide whether or not Greek life is worth the cost just for the social scene. "
    —Economics Major, University of California—Santa Cruz

" What about how much it costs to buy clothes just for rush ('recruitment' for those of you that like to be proper)! Right away I knew that joining a sorority was way beyond my student budget. Plus, I have great friends, so I don't feel like I need to join a sorority for companionship. "
    —Marketing Major, Arizona State University

" I was in a sorority for about a year and a half. I spent all of my savings on being a part of this organization. When you first enter, you spend about $600, not including monthly dues of $37. I probably spent more than $1,000 just for membership. "
    —Biology Major, University of Texas—San Antonio

" The extra fees that they don't tell you about are the initiation pin; the endless T-shirts; donations for philanthropy; social events such as mixers, semiformals, and formals; and sisterhood events. "
    —Pre-Law Major, University of Miami

" I have to pay $600 a year total for insurance, dues, and fees. However, I don't physically see where any of that money goes. Anything that we do as a fraternity requires even more money, usually an extra 20 bucks a week or so. "
—**Finance Major, Stetson University**

" In sororities, there is a semester where you are a Big Sister to a new pledge, which can cost a couple hundred dollars. "
—**Psychology Major, University of Virginia**

" I did not expect all the contributions we had to make to charity, and we got fined for everything. We also had to pay for our T-shirts, our date's T-shirts, dates to our parties, pictures, etc. It got to be very expensive and annoying. "
—**Business Major, University of Mississippi**

" Each week we had to pay at least $15 for mixers or social events on or off campus. Plus we would buy decorations, and the money would always come out of our pockets instead of the treasury. "
—**Biology Major, Pennsylvania State University**

NO GREEK? NO WAY!

There are many students for whom a Greek system is NOT a deal breaker. In other words, they apply to schools that have no Greek system to speak of, or they simply don't pay attention to which fraternities or sororities are actually available.

If it's important to you that a school has a strong Greek system, do your research before you apply to schools. This is especially true if you are looking for a particular chapter of a national organization. For example, if your mother was a Delta Delta Delta, and it's always been your dream to be one too, make sure that option is available to you.

The presence or lack of a Greek system on campus can really affect the personality of a school, so make sure you know how important it is to you.

★ TOTALLY WORTH IT! ★

Okay, you get the idea—joining a fraternity or sorority is expensive. However, for some students, the benefits far outweigh the costs. Here are ten thoughts from students who would do (and pay) it all again.

> " We used to borrow the pledges' IDs and use their unlimited dining passes to eat for free. It wasn't very nice, but it was a way to offset the cost! "
>
> **—Hospitality Business Major, Michigan State University**

" You get some great deals, and it's well worth the money. My dues were $500 per semester. I easily got that back with all the events we did. Good investment. "
—**Engineering Major, Arizona State University**

" It is the most fun I ever had in my life despite all of the expenses . . . so, if you can afford it, do it, and if you can't, there are always payment plans!! "
—**Marketing Major, Arizona State University**

" I spent approximately $5,500 a year, which sounds like a lot but ended up being cheaper than living in an apartment, paying utilities, and buying all my own food. "
—**Biology Major, University of Southern California**

" I am currently in a fraternity, and I recommend it for every incoming student. However, I am in debt a lot to my fraternity. "
—**Computer Science Major, University of Central Florida**

" Costs for social events were often paid out-of-pocket. Fortunately, our organization solicited funding from our university's student government and held fundraisers, which minimized the amount of spending required from its members. "
—**Legal Studies Major, University of Central Florida**

" A lot of money is spent on things you don't have to buy—
like T-shirts and dance favors. It's hard to resist and not
buy them because you want the souvenirs. Just plan for
those expenses as well. "
—**Biology Major, Illinois Wesleyan University**

" I pay around $1,600 a year for dues in my fraternity; how-
ever, it cuts the cost of how much I have to spend for
partying throughout the semester. "
—**Human Biology Major, Cornell University**

" I don't regret any of the money I spent during my years
in a sorority. A lot of that money was an investment in an
amazing network of women across the country who I
can call 'sister.' It wasn't cheap, but it was definitely
worth it! "
—**English Major, University of California—Santa Barbara**

" I am in a sorority, and I spend about $4,000 a year on
dues, including house bills and national dues. It would
easily cost me more than that to have an entire social
life outside of my sorority. I have absolutely no regrets—
financial or otherwise! "
—**Biochemistry Major, Oklahoma State University**

Ultimately, it is your decision about whether or not you want to participate in the Greek system at all. If you are still unsure after reading this chapter, that's ideal! It really is best to wait until you are on campus and in the position to rush or not before you make any of these decisions. Just remember, you are making this decision for yourself. During rush, it's very easy to get swept up in the "mob mentality" of everyone that wants to be a part of Greek life as if it's a necessary requirement for the college experience. It's not, so do what is best for you, and you can't go wrong.

In the next chapter, we'll cover another decision that you might have to make during school: whether or not to live off-campus.

A Whole New World: Moving Off-Campus

Yes, I was one of "those" students who spent all four years living in student housing. But it really wasn't all that bad. At the very least, housing opportunities tend to get better when you're a senior. Some schools even had on-campus "apartments" for seniors who want the feel of living off-campus without actually doing so.

Are you thinking of living off-campus? As a freshman, forget it. Most schools require (and rightfully so) that first-year students live on-campus. However, as you get older, maybe it starts to sound good—more freedom, more independence, more space, more privacy. No more bathrooms shared by 30 people, no more noise when you want quiet time to study. What could be better? ★

What you have to keep in mind is that living off-campus also means more bills, responsibilities, and liabilities. In this chapter, you'll learn about your housing options and what they can mean to you and your wallet. To give you different perspectives on living off-campus, students and recent grads will weigh in on everything from signing a lease to buying furniture.

★ SHOULD I OR SHOULDN'T I? ★

You've spent one year, maybe even two or three, in the dorms on-campus, and now you think you're ready to set out for the great beyond—an apartment off-campus that you don't have to go through the university housing office to get.

Before you make the leap, think about the pros and cons. On one hand, there's more freedom to invite your entire economics class over to complete a class project; on the other hand, there are more rooms to clean and cabinets to stock, as well as more financial responsibilities (Whose turn is it to buy toilet paper this week?). Hmm . . . to go or not to go?

Let's hear what some students and recent grads have to say about this.

Pros and Cons to Living Off-Campus

Here are ten thoughts from students who loved or hated making the move off-campus.

> " When you live off-campus, you have more space, which is a big plus. It makes things easier with roommates if you have a place to escape to. "
> —**Chemical Engineering Major, Cooper Union**

" When you live off-campus, you don't have to live on top of another person's mess. Your roommate's mess can stay behind the closed door of her own room. "
—**Journalism Major, New York University**

" Living off-campus, you finally get a sense of real independence. No more RA to solve your problems. It's just you and your roommates—and you figure it out together. "
—**Electrical Engineering Major, University of Louisville**

" Most dorms have a cleaning service for the bathrooms. In an apartment, there are often issues with cleaning the bathroom and kitchen. "
—**Labor Relations Major, Cornell University**

" Keep in mind that inevitably you will probably get on each other's nerves more but have a stronger friendship after living together. "
—**Sociology Major, Tulane University**

" The trash was an issue. In a dorm, you just have to drag it down the hall. In a house, you have to go outside and bring it to the curb on certain days. We had to assign everyone a week to do this, or our place got disgusting. "
—**Biology Major, Johns Hopkins University**

" When you live in a place with a dishwasher, it's so exciting. But most people don't realize that the clean dishes don't put themselves back in the cupboard. Nobody ever unloaded our dishwasher, so we never had plates to eat off. "
—**Sociology Major, Pennsylvania State University**

" Off-campus is another world, but it was nothing I didn't expect or wasn't ready for. I had roommates, and we were all in it together. We worked and we studied and we lived the college life . . . very well. "
—**Biology Major, Moorhead State University**

" I loved living off-campus because we had a private yard. It was so nice to have an open green space that wasn't shared by hundreds of other students! "
—**Film Studies Major, Carleton College**

" I would have rather had an RA bust up a party than the police! "
—**English Major, Tufts University**

On-Campus "Luxuries" You Take for Granted

Sure, it's easy to complain about dorm life. However, here are some things that you probably don't realize you are lucky to have:

★ **Repairs.** Not every landlord or superintendent is going to be as responsive as your school's housing and maintenance departments.

★ **RA mediation.** When you and your roommate aren't getting along, trust me, your landlord doesn't want to hear about it.

★ **Location.** Now that you are off-campus, you're going to need transportation to get yourself back on-campus.

★ **Parking.** If you have a car, is there a place to park it at your apartment, and more importantly, is there parking on-campus?

★ **Security.** Your campus had it; your new apartment might not.

★ **Furniture.** Nothing says student life like bunk beds, but hey—they were free!

★ **Knowing your neighbors.** In the dorms, everyone had their names on their doors, and you knew each other from the hall bathroom; this is not the case when you move off-campus.

★ **Utilities included.** You flip the switch and voilá, the lights go on. You will have plenty of off-campus bills for electricity, heat, hot water, Internet, cable TV, and so on.

★ **Dining halls.** When you lived on-campus, a meal was always available at the dining hall; when you live off-campus, you better learn to cook—more on that subject later!

★ **Air-conditioning and heating.** Not every apartment comes equipped with air conditioning or heating for sweltering summers and frigid winters.

★ KNOW WHAT YOU ARE GETTING INTO: A PRACTICAL CHECKLIST* ★

Renting an apartment incurs a lot of costs, which you should be aware of BEFORE you decide whether or not to move off-campus. Here are some cost-related questions to help you get the most for your money:

★ How much is monthly rent?

★ How much is the security deposit?

★ When will you get the deposit back?

★ How much money is due on the signing of the lease? First month's rent? Last month's rent? Security deposit?

---

*Adapted from Roxana Hadad, "Questions to Ask When Looking for an Apartment." *www.fastweb.com*

★ If you have roommates, do you each sign the lease? Are you each responsible for your own share of the rent, or will you be expected to cover costs if one of the roommates doesn't pay? Are there extra fees for additional roommates?

★ What date is the first rent payment due?

★ On what date is rent due after that?

★ Is there a deposit for keys or pets?

★ Which utilities are you responsible for?

★ Which utilities are included in the rent?

★ What kinds of trash removal facilities are provided for the building?

★ Are you allowed to paint or hang pictures on the wall?

★ Who is responsible for repairs to the apartment?

★ Who is responsible for repairs to the appliances?

★ CHOOSE YOUR OFF-CAMPUS ROOMIES WISELY ★

When you move off-campus, there will be no more randomly assigned roommates, and that means the choice is all yours.

However, who your off-campus roommate should be is not a choice to be made on a whim after a night with your pals at the local bar. This is a choice that will affect your entire year, so think it through before you commit! Here are some things to look out for:

★ **Focus on number one.** This is the time to be selfish. Look for people who share the same style of living as you do. If you know your friend's boyfriend is constantly going to be in your living room and that bothers you, tell her you'd rather not live with her. If your friend chugs beer for breakfast, lunch, and dinner and you don't want your home smelling like a brewery, tell him you'd rather not live with him. Just because you decide not to live with your close friends does not mean they will stop being your friends.

★ **Pick a winning number.** Think it will be fun to live with 15 of your best friends? Think again. Is this the kind of atmosphere you really want the day before you have your poli-sci final?

★ **Don't be bullied.** If your friend insists on bringing in a roommate that you don't particularly like, you are under no obligation to agree to this. Do what feels right for you.

Off-Campus Roommates: Issues and Advice

Here are ten thoughts from students who lived off-campus and still faced roommate issues. Beware of these problems and take the advice given!

> " The more people you live with, the harder it is to get everything in order. The bills are higher, and there is more stuff cluttering the apartment. "
>
> —**Law and Society Major, Oberlin College**

> " Don't live with more than two other people. Remember that you and these two other people all have girlfriends, boyfriends, and friends. Before you know it, you'll have eight people living in your house. "
>
> —**Telecommunications Major, University of Georgia**

> " When you choose a roommate, if you don't know her well and she seems a little 'off,' chances are you will find out by living with her that she is really off. Go with your instincts. "
>
> —**English Major, University of Texas—Austin**

> " I learned that you become like those around you, and since you are usually around your roommate a lot, don't live with people you don't want to be like. "
>
> —**Business Management Major, California State University**

" I rented an apartment with my two friends, and we needed another roommate to fill the fourth bedroom. One of my roommates found a girl to join us. Turns out she was a heavy drug user, had no clue how to pay bills, could not control how much she drank, and was a slob. I had trusted my roommate to make a good choice, and that was my mistake. Make sure you interview anyone who plans to live with you. "

    —Electrical Engineering Major, Texas A&M University

" Cardinal rule: Make sure your roommates can afford to live off-campus before you commit to signing a lease with them. "

    —Jurisprudence Major, Auburn University

" The solution to roommate conflicts can more often than not be resolved through the use of a simple, written contract. The parties will be bound to the terms of the contract, and should a problem arise, the possibility of being summoned to small claims court may itself provoke the other party to comply with the terms of the contract. "

    —Legal Studies Major, University of Central Florida

" My roommate is always late paying the rent, so I know I have to start asking him for the money no less than a week before it is due. "

    —English Major, Indiana University

" My roommates and I told our other roommate that if he was late with one more rent payment, we would have to kick him out of the apartment. You never want to force someone out—it's not a good feeling. But then again, it doesn't feel good either when the landlord is always calling and yelling at you over missed payments. We tried to make him understand how his neglect impacted on all of us. "
—**Mathematics Major, University of California—Davis**

" Roommate issues don't just go away when you move off-campus. You can expect all the same problems as before! "
—**English Major, Colgate University**

★ SIGNING THE LEASE ★

You and your roommates have found the perfect off-campus house. Sure, the front steps are termite ridden and the carpet is orange shag, but it's going to be your first real home on your own—as soon as you sign on the dotted line.

To rent an off-campus apartment or house, students must sign a lease with a landlord who is not affiliated with the university. A lease is a binding, legal contract outlining the rights and responsibilities of the tenants and the landlord. Every landlord has rules as to how the lease should be signed. There are usually three ways in which it is done:

★ **Only one roommate can be the primary lease-holder, with the other roommates listed as sublessees.** The primary leaseholder is solely responsible for paying the rent in full and on time, regardless of the other roommates, since the legal document is in his/her name. If one roommate doesn't pay the rent, the primary leaseholder is the only one who is liable.

★ **You and your roommates can be cotenants, which means you all sign one lease and share the responsibility equally.** If one person doesn't pay the rent, you are all responsible for coming up with the full amount. You also all share the legal responsibility in case of a problem.

★ **All the roommates sign separate leases.** Each person is responsible only for his/her share of the rent. This is your best option. If your roommate skips out, you are still responsible only for the rent amount listed on your lease. Landlords do not have to offer this, but you should always ask.

A WORD TO THE WISE

You are not a lawyer (well, at least not yet!), and neither is your roommate. Don't assume your roommate understands the fine print of the lease any better than you do. Get advice before you sign a lease and don't be afraid to negotiate any part of the lease. Ask your parents or visit your school's off-campus housing office for help.

Leases and Landlords*

Two bedrooms, a working full-sized fridge, and amazingly enough, a dishwasher—it's the perfect apartment. Now you'll have to put down a security deposit, which usually amounts to one month's rent, and you'll have to produce proof of your credit history. Remember, landlords aren't running college dorms. To get past the ingrained images of loud partying and property damage that many landlords associate with college life, check out these strategies to make yourself a better potential renter:

★ Offer a larger deposit as a show of good faith.

★ Try to get a cosigner with a good credit history (usually your parents). The cosigner is equally obligated for the rent payments and extra charges.

★ Private landlords often have less restrictive policies than large apartment complexes.

★ Prepare a set of character references and provide them up front.

*"Landlord-Tenant Fact Sheet for College Students," Springboard Non-Profit Consumer Credit Management. *www.credit.org/pdf/college_landlord_tips.pdf*

★ WHEN YOUR ROOMMATE WON'T COUGH UP THE RENT ★

It's the first of the month and—big surprise—your roommate has gone AWOL again. Now the rent is going to be late or partially unpaid, and you are put in the uncomfortable role of bill collector. Here are some ideas to get your roommate to pay up:

★ **Talk to your roommate before the situation gets out of hand.** The point of this discussion is not to humiliate your roommate but to get the rent paid. Be tactful and to the point. Do not lay blame—just say that rent is due and you are missing his check.

★ **Approach your landlord with the problem.** The landlord may be able to send your roommate a "reminder" letter.

★ **Bring in a neutral party to act as a mediator.** If it gets to the point where your roommate refuses to pay, many universities offer services for housing disputes.

★ **Expect the unexpected.** Your roommate is kicked out of college. Your roommate has an emergency at home and needs to take the year off. It happens. Students say it's best to think ahead to avoid having the rent bill arrive in your mailbox after your roommate is long gone, leaving you unable to cover her share.

★ **Make a plan.** Agree up front with your roommate that leaving voluntarily will require 30
days' notice, and he will still have to pay her
portion of the rent until he finds someone to
take her place.

★ **Advertise.** Help your out-the-door roommate
look for a new roommate. Post signs around
school and in the school newspaper.

★ **The backup.** If worse comes to worst and
your roommate skips out on you, ask your
landlord to use the absent roommate's share of
the security deposit to help pay the rent.

Roommates + Money Issues = Big Problems (Maybe)

Yes, signing a lease and having "real-world" bills to pay can
get infinitely more difficult when roommates aren't all on the
same page. Here are ten thoughts about rent and other financial problems and how to help avoid them.

" I recommend signing separate leases so that late rent
does not affect you. "
—**Political Science Major, Georgia Southern University**

" Make sure you know the penalty for having to break the lease before you commit to anything. You never know when your roommate may decide to drop out, transfer, or study abroad. "
—**Psychology Major, University of Kentucky**

" Our neighbors elected a financial chair for the house who opened a checking account for house-specific purchases. Every semester, each of the girls put in a couple hundred dollars that they used to pay the bills and recreational expenses. If the account got low, they all chipped in a little more. "
—**Economics Major, Bucknell University**

" We had a running list of extra expenses that one person or another ended up paying for—like beer for parties, cleaning supplies, etc.—and at the end of the year, the expenses were totaled and checks were written so that the financial responsibility evened out. "
—**Political Science Major, Brown University**

" Getting everyone to put in their share of the security deposit was tricky. No one wanted to hand over money they might never see again because of someone else's mistake. "
—**Jurisprudence Major, Auburn University**

" My roommate wouldn't pay the rent so I had to take her to court. Can you believe she countersued me for emotional distress? "
—Film Studies Major, Carleton College

" You have to remember to sit down with your roommates and collect money for rent. You don't want to end up paying a late fee or facing eviction! "
—Speech Communications Major, Kansas State University

" My roommates and I used to have problems with rent checks. Some people would get mad if they didn't write their check in time for it to clear in the other person's account. Finally, we had rent 'due' to each other a week in advance so that there were no bounced rent checks. "
—Elementary Education Major, Saint Vincent College

" If you want something done right, do it yourself. I loved being in charge of the financial matters in the house because I knew I could get everyone to cough up what they owed. I was not going to put up with late fees or other penalties when it came to paying rent and other bills. "
—Italian Studies Major, New York University

" Know what money is due up front when you sign your lease. You may think $500 a month is a breeze until you realize that you have to come up with $1,500 (first, last, one-month security) just to get your name on the lease! "
—**English Major, Duke University**

★ PAYING THE BILLS ★

You and your roommates are like peas in a pod—you all like to study in complete silence, all are a bit messy, and all like to throw a great party. But on the first and the fifteenth of every month when the stack of bills arrives, the similarities end. One roommate is diligent about paying on time, one roommate needs constant reminders, and one roommate is forever broke. That's when the hostility and resentment begin to grow, often resulting in roommates arguing over how much to contribute or what each person's share is. Who knew that ten-minute hot showers were a true luxury?

Here are some tips to follow so that paying bills runs as smoothly as possible*:

1. **Create a system for utilities.**
   ★ If possible, find an apartment that includes utilities as part of the monthly rent. The fewer bills, the fewer conflicts.

*Source: "How to Handle Roommate Finances." *www.nefcu.com*

★ When it comes to heat and water bills, it is often simpler to agree to spilt these bills evenly rather than haggle over usage. Agree to turn out the lights and turn off the water when you are not using it.

★ If you don't want the hassle of splitting each bill evenly, guesstimate the bills so that each person has close to an equal financial responsibility each month. For example, if the heating bill is $200 and the water bill is $100 and the telephone bill is $100, then one roommate is responsible for paying the first bill and the other roommate is responsible for the other two.

2. **Address questions up front.**

★ What will happen if one of you does not have enough money to pay the rent or a utility bill one month?

★ How will late charges be handled?

★ Whose name will the bills be registered under?

Calling Judge Judy!

Usually, you'll be able to resolve any conflicts with your roommates by being honest and clear about what needs to be paid and when and what items can be shared. But every once in a while, a roommate comes along who won't change her financially devious habits. Here are some resources for dealing with a wayward roommate:

★ **Look into the legal side of things.** It might seem extreme, but don't rule out written contracts or agreements stating rules for paying bills or buying groceries. Showing your roommate that you're serious about keeping things straight might just be the kick in the pants she needs to shape up.

★ **Get out while you can.** If things are really bad, there's no reason to watch your savings dwindle as your roommate eats all your food and rings up the phone bill.

★ **Go to a dean or financial officer for advice.** Sharing conflicts between roommates isn't anything new to college advisors, so you can benefit from their wisdom and experience.

Bills, Bills, Bills

When you live in a dorm, it's easy to take things like electricity, Internet hookup, and air-conditioning for granted. Here are ten thoughts from students about all the bills associated with living off-campus.

" When the rent and other bills arrive, I open them immediately and post them with the return envelope on the bulletin board in our kitchen. Everyone drops her check into the envelope, and she has to do it ten days before the bill is due. "
—**International Relations Major, Bucknell University**

" If a bill was late because of a particular roommate, that person would have to pay all the late fees. "
—**Engineering Major, Georgia Southern University**

" My roommate would leave our bills in a stack and pay them a month after they were due. To try and rectify the problem, I left her notes on the fridge when each bill was due. "
—**English Major, University of Texas—Austin**

" It's better to have a quick, uncomfortable conversation about bills and money than to have a series of heated, difficult conversations later on. "
—**Women's Studies Major, Smith College**

" One year I lived with my boyfriend and his friend. I was the only one with a checking account, a credit card, and a driver's license. I paid the bills and collected cash. It didn't work too well, and to this day I am still paying off the debt from those deadbeats. You learn the hard way. "

—Biology Major, Moorhead State University

" There are a million and one bills you have to pay! No one ever told me I would have to pay to breathe my own air! "

—Biology Major, Temple University

" We had some trouble with the heating bill being so high. People in the house kept playing with the thermostat. Someone would put it higher, and then someone else would lower it. Last month, we paid more than $200. That was a pain. We talked about it and agreed to set it at 68 degrees and no one's touched it, and we can't blame anyone for it. "

—Criminal Justice Major, Indiana University—Bloomington

" You should know up front that if a bill is in your name and it doesn't get paid, it will damage your credit. "

—Government Major, Connecticut College

" It's hard to split a gas/electric/cable bill with house-mates. You just need to elect one person to handle it and get people to write him a check and make sure they pay promptly. Individual stuff gets too confusing. "

—**History Major, Washington and Lee University**

" My roommates and I used to fight over every single bill we had. They had to determine down to the penny what we owed. Phone bills were the worst. We had to sit and go through every phone call to figure out exactly who owed what, including tax and extras like call waiting. Sharing groceries was a problem too. Some people would get mad if they went to get something and there was none left. We avoided this by buying our own gro-ceries and never using one another's things. "

—**Elementary Education Major, Saint Vincent College**

HOUSE PARTIES

Congratulations! You and your roommate(s) are actually getting along and want to throw a social event together. Here are a few pointers to make sure that the party runs smoothly—and that there are no hard feelings when it's all over. Decide together:

★ A date that works for both of you. Be understanding—if your roommate has a midterm the next day or a huge paper to write, no party.

★ Who will be invited. Do you really need to invite your acquaintance from Chem 207 when you know your roommate can't stand him? Think about the greater good.

★ How big the party will be. In some cases, size does matter. Don't let the saying "The more the merrier" lead to having your party shut down before it really gets going.

★ The confines of the party. Discuss if any rooms or items will be off-limits during the party. Respect your roommate's requests.

★ Money matters. Agree on how much you each want to chip in for alcohol or soda and make sure there are no hard feelings afterward.

★ The morning after. Agree to clean up together—no matter if you're hung over, if you've hooked up, or if the smell of half-eaten pizza disgusts you.

★ FOOD, GLORIOUS FOOD! ★

That room where all the pots and pans are kept is called your kitchen—you know, the place where you SHOULD be making your meals. Living off-campus means you probably aren't as reliant on the dining hall and meal plan as you used to be. Cooking at home is a great way to keep food in your stomach and money in your wallet.

Saving money starts with being supermarket savvy. Here are a few things to keep in mind:

★ **Make a list of what you need for the week and stick to it.** Otherwise, you'll probably decide you need way more items than you actually do—and may duplicate things you already have!

★ **Don't go to the store when you are hungry.** Huge steaks and store-made cupcakes will find their way into your cart, and you will wind up spending more money than you need to.

★ **Shop for nonperishable items like canned vegetables, rice, and crackers.** If you buy too many fresh items, they'll most likely go bad before you eat them.

★ **Coupons, coupons, coupons, and club cards!** Why pay full price when you don't have to?

If what is stumping you is what to make, here are some student-friendly suggestions:

★ **Barbecued chicken.** Don't have a barbecue? No problem! Put two chicken breasts on a piece of tin foil. Smother with barbecue sauce. Seal up the foil and put in the oven. Set oven to 350 degrees and cook for 45 minutes.

★ **Beans and rice.** Warm up a can of kidney beans in a pan with some oil or butter. Boil a helping of minute rice. Combine. Stir in some salsa. Grate in some cheddar cheese. Eat either with or without tortillas. (You can add any number of items to this dish—lettuce, sautéed onions, sour cream—but these are the basic ingredients.)

★ **Pizza muffins.** Spread tomato sauce and a slice of cheese on top of an English muffin. Toast or bake for a few minutes. Instant pizza!

★ **Pasta with asparagus.** Cut one bunch of asparagus into bite-sized pieces. Cook in boiling water. Drain. Cook one-half pound penne in boiling water. Drain. Combine asparagus and penne. Coat with butter and Parmesan cheese. Season with salt and pepper.

★ **Quesadillas.** All you need are tortillas, cheese, and a microwave. Dress them up with whatever ingredients you want.

★ **Stir-fry.** The beauty of stir-fry is that you can cut up any meat and/or vegetables you want to throw in. Just make sure there's some olive oil in the pan first. If you want to be fancy, buy stir-fry sauce or soy sauce to toss in at the end of the cooking. Serve over rice.

★ **Frittatas.** Melt some butter in a pan. Crack two eggs into the pan and stir them up. As soon as the eggs start to solidify, throw in grated cheese and any cut-up vegetables you wish. Finish cooking the eggs and slide the frittata onto a plate.

★ **Burgers.** Is anything easier than cooking burgers on the George Foreman grill? The secret is to season the meat with salt, pepper, and steak sauce (if you have it) before forming the hamburger.

College Gourmet

Here are ten thoughts from students who maybe didn't eat gourmet but definitely dined on a budget.

" Ramen noodles cost about 50 cents a metric ton. You can't go wrong with ramen noodles.**"**

—**Microbiology Major, University of South Florida—Tampa**

" Three words: beans and rice. "
—Italian Studies Major, New York University

" Cooking for yourself is not always time effective, but if you can find someone else to help you and to share with, it makes it cheaper and more enjoyable. "
—Economics Major, Ohio State University

" I saved money on dinner by having an apartment with a decent-sized kitchen. If my roommates and I ever didn't have enough money to scrounge together a decent meal, we just invited all of our friends over and told them each to bring a course for the meal. We wound up with plenty of wacky college kitchen hijinks as well as saving a ton of money by cooking for as many as 20 people with each of us spending less than $10! "
—Communications Major, Drexel University

" The 'trick' is to get food from the grocery store and not the fast-food joint. The value of a dollar goes much further when you prepare a meal yourself (rather than purchase it prepared), not to mention that homemade meals can be much healthier than fast food. "
—Legal Studies Major, University of Central Florida

" Every grocery store in town had flyers in the local newspaper stating all of the great sales on food. Watching and partaking in this shopping strategy allowed anybody to eat everything their body needed as long as they had a freezer to stock up. "

—**Political Science Major, Central Washington University**

" I guess I never took into account how eating out really does add up. At times, it's just inconvenient to go through the trouble of making food—especially when you're pressed for time—so you usually end up finding yourself scarfing down something at the nearest fast-food chain. I usually try to avoid this by making a whole lot of food on the weekend that can last me through the week. "

—**Psychology Major, University of California—Davis**

" If you have a car, don't get delivery. "

—**International Studies Major, Northwestern University**

" Make sure that you are friends with students who have parents in the area, so that you get invited over to their house for dinner. The benefits don't end there. Snacks, free laundry . . . "

—**Biology Major, Cornell University**

" Learn how to cook or get a roommate who can. "
—Commercial Graphics Major, Pittsburgh State University

★ FURNITURE ★

Some off-campus apartments come with furniture included, but many do not. What happens when one roommate is happy with an overturned box as a coffee table and a couch with the stuffing hanging out, and the other prefers coordinating birch furniture from Ikea with matching slipcovers? You're going to have to find a happy medium.

If you are both broke but still want more than milk crates as chairs, check out *www.craigslist.org* where you can find anything from beds to couches for free. If there's nothing like this in your area, keep reading to hear some creative solutions for furnishing your apartment.

Stocking Your New Home

If your apartment is unfurnished, you're going to need a lot of stuff to fill the empty space. Here are ten thoughts from students and recent grads on how to fill your new home as well as what to do when you all move out.

" Make sure you keep all your receipts for furniture and write everything down, so at the end of the year you have a record of what the item costs and how much each person contributed. "
    —**Chemistry Major, University of the Pacific**

" Large purchases like furniture are difficult to divide because the question of who gets to keep the shared purchase inevitably comes up at the end of the year. I avoided this by just buying the whole thing myself or letting my roommate buy it. "
    —**Political Science Major, Pennsylvania State University**

" If we had to buy furniture for our apartment, we would split the money evenly, then at the end of the year if someone wanted to buy it, they could—or we would try to sell it and split the money. "
    —**Environmental Studies Major, University of Colorado—Boulder**

" Five of us lived together in a house after freshman year. We pooled everything left in our parents' homes—old sofas, broken chairs, cracked plates. The place was bursting with remnants of our attics at home. "
    —**Economics Major, University of North Carolina**

" When buying things for the apartment like Internet hubs, it's hard to split the cost because only one person will get to keep it in the end. But I don't think that person should pay for the whole thing either. A resolution would be that the person who gets to keep it pays a little more, but the others also pay some of the cost. "
—**Integrative Biology Major, University of California—Berkeley**

" There is the issue of food, but I always had a contribute-as-much-as-you-eat attitude, and we didn't have too many problems. This does become troublesome if you have a mooching roommate, but then if that's the case, you've probably got bigger problems. "
—**English Major, University of Puget Sound**

" There were issues with roommates where I would end up buying more supplies at times. We basically assigned who bought what and came out with a reasonable agreement. We knew what we each needed to buy, and it was never a problem. Communication is very important. "
—**Psychology Major, New York University**

" Make sure that if you do split a large purchase, you have a contract or written agreement so that there can be no argument about what will happen to the merchandise when school ends or someone leaves. "
—**Biology Major, North Park University**

" My roommate would always go to the grocery store with us and never buy anything because she didn't have the money. She would say she didn't want to eat anything. Then when she was hungry, she would help herself to our food. "

—**Marketing Major, Quinnipiac University**

" At the end of the year, we had a lottery for splitting all our major purchases. We put our names in a hat and drew for things like the couch, the TV, and other major furniture items. Of course, if you won something, it was great. Even if you didn't, at least you know that you had an equal chance of 'winning' something as the other person. "

—**Art History Major, University of California—Davis**

INSURANCE

Consider getting renter's insurance for your apartment. You can get this from a housing insurance agency, among other places. Renter's insurance covers theft and the damage that can happen to your belongings in a fire or flood.

★ THINK IT ALL THROUGH ★

You probably aren't aware of everything that will change when you move off-campus. Here are ten thoughts about things you might not have considered but should think twice about before you move.

" When you live off-campus, there are excessive amounts of bills that you don't consider when living in a dorm. Every time one gets paid, another one shows up. You and your roommates will be forever talking about money and who pays what part of what bill."
    —Marketing Major, Arizona State University

" The need to borrow a car increases when one lives off-campus. Make some sort of arrangement to borrow your roommate's car but make sure that you are respectful and you offer to pay for the gas and repairs."
    —Political Science Major, Washington University—St. Louis

" If you have cars, take turns with the only available parking space."
    —Biology Major, University of California—Irvine

" When I moved off-campus, I didn't even think about having to park both at home AND on campus. I was late to a lot of classes because I was searching for parking, and I got a lot of tickets when I just took the first spot I could find, even if it was illegal! "
    —Anthropology Major, Emory University

" If you are a big TV watcher, you should get your own TV for your bedroom. There is no chance that you and your roommate will always want to watch all the same shows. "
    —Journalism Major, Ohio University

" I didn't know how hard it is to get a landlord to give back the security deposit. Keep really good records and make sure you document damage already in the apartment, or the landlord will stick you with it. "
    —Public Relations Major, Brigham Young University

" Last year, we had to pay for the 'Common Building Damages.' This meant that everyone who lived in the building had to split the cost of things like cleanup after parties, missing doorbell ringers, damage to the siding of the building—things that we did not do. It was really annoying, but legally, they could do that. "
    —Journalism Major, Syracuse University

" Trash bags are pretty expensive. That's something you take for granted in the dorms! "
—Physics Major, State University of New York—Binghamton

" When we moved off-campus, all my roommates agreed to buy a puppy. My advice—never get a puppy in the winter, two weeks before finals, that needs to be house-broken and walked constantly, because none of you will want to be responsible for it! "
—English Major, Tufts University

" When I got my first off-campus apartment, I was really excited about getting a pet. Pets are a bad idea. Not only is it hard to find a place that allows pets of any kind, but think about all the holidays when you will need to find a pet sitter! "
—Computer Science Major, Union College

If and when you do get your first "real" apartment, it is certainly an exciting time, whether you are still in college or you are a recent graduate. Knowing what you are getting yourself into will make all the difference, so do your research as best you can.

And so you've made it this far . . . from your first day on campus to your first off-campus apartment. In the next and last chapter, we'll offer some parting words of wisdom.

★ N I N E ★

Last but Not Least

Well done! You've made it this far in *College Unzipped: An All-Access, Backstage Pass into College Life, from All-Nighters and Exam Nail Biters, to Tuition Fees and Getting Your Degree.* You're now a near-expert on dorm life, roommate issues, Greek life, off-campus living, and the all-important college hookups. But as you will learn, in college and in life, you should always expect the unexpected. There's no manual to having a great four years, there's no to-do list for college, and there's definitely no "right" way to get yourself to graduation day.

Since every experience is unique, this chapter partially abandons the ten thoughts "rule" and gives you any number of quotes on other college life topics. As always, don't take these thoughts at face value. Although they speak to some universal truths, know that your college experience will be exactly what YOU make of it. ★

★ DON'T SWEAT THE SMALL STUFF ★

In college, I was not just type A, I was type A+. Everything I did (especially academically) had to be done perfectly. For this reason, stress was my security blanket. I'm still prone to high levels of stress, but I definitely learned some great ways to minimize it or eliminate it completely. Trust me, you won't remember what you got on your midterm exam in Economics 101 by the time you graduate, so take my advice and don't put too much unnecessary pressure on yourself.

Keep reading to learn the ways some students handled stress in college.

Proven Stress Relievers

Here are ten thoughts from current students and recent grads on the best ways to get a handle on your stress levels.

" Sleep does wonders. "
—**Engineering Sciences Major, Dartmouth College**

" Cleaning. Oddly enough, my favorite time to clean was when I had big assignments due. "
—**Public Relations Major, University of Georgia**

" Exercising . . . plus it kept off the freshman 15. "
—Science Major, Southern Illinois University—Edwardsville

" Even socializing at the library during study breaks helps a lot! "
—Political Science Major, University of North Florida

" Having water fights in the hall and playing in the snow. "
—Biology Major, Midland Lutheran College

" Going to the coffee house for a cup of coffee and chatting with friends, or playing guitar and writing songs with my friends. "
—Music/Economics Major, Lake Forest College

" Long walks through the safe neighborhoods around campus. You get to dabble in the old family-centered life you miss, and you get to free your mind from the worries that surround you when you're on campus. "
—Psychology Major, Xavier University

" I loved to lie around in the grass under a tree on a nice sunny day. It's the best way to get your mind off those challenging assignments that lie ahead. "
—English Major, University of Maryland—College Park

" Watching soap operas. I even went so far as to plan one semester so no classes would interfere with my favorite soap! "
—Legal Studies Major, Quinnipiac University

" Video games are a great way to work out your aggressions. "
—Microbiology Major, Indiana University

★ LIVING IN INFAMY ★

Embarrassing stuff is going to happen throughout your life. Maybe you already had a mortifying moment in high school. Well, look at it this way, when you go away to college, no one knows you as "the girl who burped out loud during Monday assembly." Just accept that something embarrassing may happen, but that you WILL be able to live it down. Have a sense of humor, and you will be set to survive whatever happens at college. If something particularly mortifying happens, take comfort in the fact that no one back home ever has to know about it!

Most Embarrassing Moments

Because college has no shortage of embarrassing moments, we're now offering you 20 thoughts on cringe-worthy moments and, more importantly, how to keep them in perspective.

" College is nothing but a list of embarrassing experiences. Get ready to enjoy them all! "
   —**Political Science Major, Indiana University**

" My most embarrassing moment was coming home on New Year's Eve and having my roommate inform me that my shiny silver pants had a huge rip in the butt. I had been out all night like that! "
   —**Pre-Law Major, University of Illinois—Urbana-Champaign**

" I got caught streaking by a police officer . . . he let me go, though. "
   —**Psychology Major, University of Virginia**

" For crew initiation, I had to wear the same outfit for a whole week and then sing and dance in the cafeteria!"
—**Biology Major, Georgetown University**

" I slipped on some ice on the sidewalk in front of about 200 people, all gathered together because they knew about the ice patch and were waiting for people to slip."
—**Linguistics Major, Brigham Young University**

" One night at a party, some friends convinced a girl I had never laid eyes on before that I was in love with her. Needless to say, when she confronted me about it in front of a bunch of people, I wanted to crawl into a hole."
—**History Major, University of Massachusetts**

" I was showing a group of students and their parents around campus, and I slipped and fell down a massive flight of wet stairs. Afterward, I triumphantly got up and yelled 'I'm okay!' Nevertheless, it was embarrassing."
—**Religious Studies Major, Brown University**

" I accidentally pulled out a plug in a public computer room, and every computer shut down. It happened before final exams, when papers are due! "
—**Biology Major, State University of New York—Buffalo**

" My freshman year, I was at a party during the winter and tripped headlong into a swimming pool. Mind you, I was sober. "
—**Government Major, University of Texas—Austin**

" I passed out during a fire drill and had to be carried upstairs when it was over. "
—**Neuroscience Major, University of Rochester**

" My most embarrassing experience was when I realized how thin the walls are in the dorms and that everyone could hear me singing in my room. "
—**Spanish Major, University of Wisconsin—Madison**

" First day of classes. Freshman year. A 75-person lecture. I tipped over in my desk as I was reaching for my pen. Everyone, including the professor, laughed at me. "
—**Chemical Engineering Major, University of Virginia**

" The lab gloves in my basic chemistry class were slippery, and I dropped a bottle, sending a very strong base flying everywhere. They called the fire department and made me stand in the chemical shower in the middle of class! When they finally took me to the ER, they said I was fine and released me. But I made that evening's news! "
   —**Ecology Major, University of California—Davis**

" I meant to send a romantic e-mail to my boyfriend and accidentally sent it to a professor instead. (The professor's e-mail address was listed underneath my boyfriend's in my e-mail address book.) I got an A in the class! "
   —**History Major, Rutgers University**

" I sat in the wrong classroom for about 20 minutes before realizing it was a graduate class, and then I made a not-so-nonchalant exit. "
   —**American Studies Major, University of Notre Dame**

" A bird pooped on my leg during orientation week. It was the first time I had met anyone at school, and for the rest of the week, everyone knew me as the girl the bird pooped on. "
   —**Engineering Major, St. Louis University**

" I fell asleep in my friends' room, and they put a large plastic rooster head in bed next to me and took a large color photo. "
—**French Major, Cornell University**

" I walked in on my roommate not once, not twice, but three times when she was naked with her boyfriend. She didn't have a signal system. "
—**English Major, University of California—Davis**

" Sometimes you just gotta take it and not be embarrassed. It makes life a lot easier. "
—**Physics Major, Grossmont College**

" Hey, it's college. NOTHING is embarrassing. "
—**Biology Major, Spring Hill College**

★ RELISH ALL THE GOOD STUFF ★

It can't be said enough—college is where you will have some of the best, funniest, and most memorable moments of your life. Be sure to balance studying with making friends and making memories. There's a reason people are so nostalgic for their college days!

Fondest Memories

Here are ten thoughts on some of the most memorable events of these students' college careers.

" A group of us burned our notes from our organic chemistry class after a miserable semester. It was good riddance and a great stress reliever. "
        —Environmental Studies Major, Washington College

" Last year I lived in an on-campus apartment with two other girls. We, along with the people in the apartment next to us, threw a Mardi Gras party. We handed out flyers all over campus. The place was so packed that you couldn't move, and the cops broke it up within the first hour. It was quite a success for those few minutes, though! "
        —Biology Major, College of William & Mary

" Road trips are great. I'll never forget all the road trips I've taken with different girlfriends at college—Omaha, Twin Cities, little hick towns with divey bars. It's all been a blast. "
        —Biochemistry Major, Cornell College

" We don't get much snow in Cincinnati, but during the winter of my sophomore year, we had a big storm. I was the resident assistant for our basketball team, and many of them were out-of-towners who had never seen snow. We all bundled up, went outside, and started an enormous snowball fight along with the residents of the dorm next door. It was great! "

—**Psychology Major, Xavier University**

" My most memorable experience was graduation day. I was late to the ceremony and ended up being the last person in my school to walk into NYU's graduation in Washington Square Park. Among the thousands of students that were there, I somehow managed to meet up with my best friends in—yes, in—the fountain after it was all over. It's still one of my favorite memories. "

—**Italian Studies Major, New York University**

" My most memorable experience was getting a 4.0 GPA for a semester. I had never done that in high school, and it was one of my goals. "

—**Accounting Major, Washington University—St. Louis**

" I passed a test for which I had studied for two weeks straight. It was a big deal because the test was given by a professor who was notorious for his detailed tests. I felt great, and I learned what I was capable of doing. "

—**English Major, Morehouse College**

❝ My most memorable experience was the day I finished up my last term paper and handed it to my professor. As I put it in his hands, he said to me very calmly, 'You are now a graduate.' ❞

—Political Science Major, State University of New York— Buffalo

❝ At graduation I was honored with an award named after a late professor who meant the world to me. ❞

—Environmental Policy Major, Wells College

❝ My most memorable moment was walking out of my last exam my senior year. It was bittersweet. I wanted to stay because I loved the life . . . but I knew it was time to move on, and I was proud of what I had done. ❞

—History Major, University of Massachusetts

★ DON'T LET IT ALL PASS YOU BY ★

While high school may have seemed like an eternity, college is the opposite. The time that elapses between freshman orientation and graduation day seems like four weeks, not four years! Enjoy everything while it lasts, because it will be over before you know it and you don't want to have any regrets. Keep reading to learn of things other people regretted so that maybe you won't have to.

Biggest Regrets

Here are ten thoughts from students on their biggest regrets during college. Take their advice so you don't end up wishing you had done things differently.

" I didn't have enough fun while I was in college. I found the perfect balance of work and play too late. Find it early!"
—**Psychology Major, University of Georgia**

" I regret that I only truly enjoyed my last year of college. I appreciated where I was and who I was with only when I knew it wasn't going to last."
—**Cognitive Science Major, University of Virginia**

" My biggest regret is that I didn't take advantage of more free concerts, speeches, and events."
—**Biology Major, Indiana University**

" I regret not taking advantage of everything college had to offer. There were so many speakers and colloquiums, but I was always too busy or too tired. I wish I'd experienced more of the diversity and intellectual environment. "
—**Neuroscience Major, University of Rochester**

" My biggest regret is blowing off fun plans in order to get work done. Yes, schoolwork is very important, but there are a lot of other experiences at college that will stay with you forever. "
—**Government Major, University of Virginia**

" My biggest regret was getting tied down with a boyfriend for two years—my friends slipped away. "
—**Chemistry Major, John Carroll University**

" I didn't meet enough upperclassmen when I was a freshman. I lived in the all-freshman dorm and had automatic friends, so I didn't branch out much until the second semester when I was involved in a play. I missed out on a lot of car trips that way! "
—**Biology Major, Oberlin College**

" My biggest regret is not transferring out when I had the chance. Although I have met a few wonderful people, I spent four years of my life in a place that I didn't like very much, where I did not fit in, and where there were very few people I could relate to. If you feel by midyear of your freshman year that you made the wrong decision about which college to attend . . . leave! There's no sense in spending four years of your life being unhappy. It is a pain to fill out transfer applications, but do it on the chance that the next place will be better. "

    —English Major, Millsaps College

" My biggest regret was not going to class a lot my freshman year. I thought that I didn't need to go to class since I didn't have to, so I usually didn't, and I suffered the consequences! "

    —Psychology Major, University of Illinois—Urbana-Champaign

" I regret not changing my major. I thought I had to know what I wanted to do when I got to college, so I stuck with it even though I wasn't satisfied, because I was afraid of uncertainty. "

    —Gender Studies Major, Northwestern University

★ THE NEXT STEP ★

No, the point here is not to help you plan out the rest of your life. The point is only to remind you that YES, there is life AFTER college. Enjoy your life as a student, but try to keep the longer-term future in perspective.

Preparing for the Future

Since we are talking about your life AFTER COLLEGE, here are 20 thoughts on preparing for your future.

> " I always thought that when you were a senior, recruiters flocked to your door and begged you to sign on for a position at some company relating exactly to your major. Apparently, that's not what happens. "
> —**Biology Major, University of Central Florida**

> " I was overprepared for the job market. I had internships during my summer and January breaks. I also completed a senior thesis and attended conferences so that I had completed a major piece of writing and had presentation experience. It was not a terrible position to be in, but it made me wish I had taken more time to have fun during school. "
> —**Environmental Science Major, Wells College**

" I wish I had done a better internship during my senior year or summer breaks. Internships help you figure out what jobs are out there and what you need to know to get them. "
    —**Environmental Studies Graduate, Emory & Henry College**

" Get good internships! This is the only time you will be given responsibility without having any experience. Employers and graduate schools will look favorably on these internships. "
    —**Political Science Major, University of California—San Diego**

" I wish I hadn't concentrated so much on getting involved in extracurricular activities to pad my résumé; it ended up costing me a better GPA. "
    —**Biology Major, College of Charleston**

" I wish that I had gotten a minor in Spanish. Being able to speak two languages makes you a better commodity in the job market. "
    —**Criminal Justice Major, Westchester University**

" Employers and grad schools want to work with people who show some level of focus, not people who dabble in a little bit of everything. "
    —**Marketing Major, Howard University**

" If you think there's a chance you're going to go to graduate school, making academic contacts early becomes important, especially when the time comes for you to get recommendations. "
    —Spanish Major, Loyola College

" Employers want to know what your experience is, not what grades you got. Graduate school is a balance between the two. They want to know that you challenged yourself with the classes you picked and that you participated in something besides school. "
    —Law and Society Major, University of California—Irvine

" I wish I had networked more with alumni and attended graduate school workshops put on by the university. "
    —Political Economy of Industrial Societies Major, University of California—Berkeley

" I should have taken advantage of the mock interview sessions offered by the career center. "
    —Art and Design Major, Lagrange College

" I wish I had attended more optional lectures about applying to graduate schools. "
    —Clarinet Performance Major, Vassar College

" I wish I had taken advantage of the career center. I would have been exposed to more companies and had more opportunities to practice interviews. "
    —**Microbiology Major, Indiana University**

" I wish I had taken a class on writing résumés and cover letters, job strategies, and interviewing skills. I graduated thinking I would have no problem getting a job, but it's a lot harder than I thought—I wish someone had prepared me better for that reality. "
    —**Criminal Justice Major, Viterbo University**

" I should have studied the job market more carefully and found out what exactly it is that I wanted to do. I should have taken advantage of alumni networking and professors to talk about what certain jobs are like. "
    —**International Studies Major, Brigham Young University**

" I wish I had known what classes would be best to take for my major and the career I wanted to go into. "
    —**Biology Major, Clemson University**

" I wish I had taken the GRE waaaaay earlier. I should have taken a prep class back in the early part of my junior year. I'm currently jobless and frantically applying to grad schools. "
    —**Psychology Major, University of Michigan—Ann Arbor**

" I wish I had worked hard all four years. It is tough to change your GPA drastically. It seems to go down more quickly than it goes up. "
          —**Sociology Major, University of Wisconsin—Madison**

" Get your recommendations right after you finish a course with a professor, as opposed to senior year when you need them. That way, you're fresh in their minds. "
          —**Psychology Major, Connecticut College**

" I took college seriously, and I got into law school and I landed a great job. The people who thought college was something they did not have to work at are still looking for a job and did not make it to graduate school. "
          —**Criminology Major, University of California—Irvine**

★ FINAL WORDS OF WISDOM ★

Cue the melodrama!

This is it. Everything you've read thus far all comes down to this.

Of course it doesn't! However, this book would not be complete without more sage advice about college and what it can mean to you. Here are the final thoughts of *College Unzipped: An All-Access, Backstage Pass into College Life, from All-Nighters and Exam Nail Biters, to Tuition Fees and Getting Your Degree.* Enjoy!

" Now is your time to live. "

> —**International Studies Major, Northwestern University**

" Spontaneity is the key to life. College is the last time you will have the freedom to ditch a Friday class to go snowboarding or skip your 12:40 to meet the boys down at the local DIVE for wings and beer. Take advantage. "

> —**Pre-Medicine Major, Arizona State University**

" You don't have to come out of college with a 4.0 GPA, but it will get you a lot further in life than a 2.0. Balance your time accordingly. "

> —**Biology Major, College of Charleston**

" Don't be misled by the crazy college life you see in movies and on television. They only show the fun and not the consequences. "

> —**Chinese Language Major, University of California—Irvine**

" Be open to friendships with all different types of people.
It makes life much more interesting than hanging out
with people just like you. "
—**Biochemistry Major, University of California—Los Angeles**

" Keep an open mind. Just because you've never done it,
seen it, or tried it before doesn't make it bad. "
—**History Major, Indiana University—Bloomington**

" Remember that you have limits. Don't overdo it. "
—**Government Major, Dartmouth College**

" Go to class. It doesn't matter how hung over you are, or
if you haven't showered, or if you didn't do the work—
go. You'll thank yourself later. "
—**Legal Studies Major, University of Massachusetts—Amherst**

" Take the time to LISTEN; you'll learn more. "
—**Spanish Major, University of Texas—Austin**

" Buy a 24-hour planner. Trust me, it'll be the best $25 you
spend each year. "
—**Linguistics Major, New York University**

" Customize your education to something that you will enjoy. No one else will tell you how to make the best out of your education—you have to do that yourself! "

—Political Science Major, University of California—San Diego

" Don't pretend to be something you're not. Don't do things just to fit in. Be yourself. There are countless others who will find you fun and exciting just for being YOU. "

—Chemistry Major, Denison University

" Learn as quickly as possible that you don't know everything. It will make you more open to learning all the things that you really don't have a clue about! "

—Anthropology Major, Emory University

" While in college, you mature and grow outside the classroom far more than you grow inside the classroom. The relationships you make and the people you meet will be the memories that you carry with you forever. It's not how you studied for that big test, it's how you and your friends were able to drive to Atlantic City the night before the test and study on the way there and back and still do fine on the exam. "

—Nutritional Sciences Major, Pennsylvania State University

" Don't take yourself too seriously. If something seems like a huge failure, very urgent, or stressful, take a step back and look at how important that small event is compared to the whole picture. What seems incredibly important at the time usually isn't worth stressing yourself out about. "
    —Biomedical Sciences Major, Marquette University

" I learned that what you accomplish doesn't create who you are, but who you are drives your accomplishments. "
    —English and Music Major, College of William & Mary

" Act confident and you'll feel confident! "
    —Pre-Medicine Major, Pennsylvania State University

" Depend on yourself. Even with the strongest support system, you still need to rely on Number One to get things done. "
    —Psychology Major, Colby-Sawyer College

" Decisions you make for yourself, by yourself, make you the happiest. "
    —Government/German Studies Major, Smith College

" It's not so much WHAT you learn in college that helps you in life, it's learning HOW to think that will help you out in the long run. College doesn't teach you the solution to everything, but it teaches you how to come up with a solution on your own. "
      —**Biometry and Statistics Major, Cornell University**

" I became very humble in college. I realized that there was actually very little about the world that I knew and have accepted that as a starting point to a postcollege life of learning. "
      —**English Major, Connecticut College**

" If you want to follow your passions, you will have to sacrifice a lot, but in the end you will be happier than the people who are just out for the money. "
      —**Biology Major, Georgetown University**

" Don't cheat or take the easy road. You will have to struggle for most of the good things in life. Work hard and be proud of your work product. "
      —**Political Science Major, University of California—San Diego**

" I learned that having a role model or mentor helps you get through the day. "
—**Biological Sciences Major, University of California—Davis**

" Who you know is more important than what you know. "
—**Biology Major, Indiana University**

" Make the best of things and don't be a whiner. No matter how bad things look or how stressed out you are, things will work out one way or another. Things will work out the quickest if you keep your cool! "
—**International Studies Major, Brigham Young University**

" Reinventing myself and finding new people to be friends with was the best part. "
—**Psychology Major, University of San Francisco**

" Take risks. Go out on a limb. Don't be afraid to do things you, your friends, and maybe even your family don't think you're capable of. Put everything on the line so you can find out what you're really capable of and who you really are. "
—**Philosophy Major, St. John's College—Annapolis**

" It's important to take time and be the stereotype . . .
dye your hair blue, be a pseudo-hippie, protest stuff . . .
it'll never be as socially acceptable as it is now. "
        —Biochemistry Major, University of California—San Diego

" Cherish the time you have in college. Like our parents
say, college is the best time of your life. It is very true. "
        —Biology Major, Xavier University

" Be true to yourself and live like there is no tomorrow. "
        —Philosophy Major, College of William & Mary

" Find yourself. It'll be the most important thing you'll do. "
        —Psychology Major, University of Illinois—Chicago

" You'll meet many different types of people in college.
Take advantage of the freedom to express who
you are, and learn from those who are different
from you. "
        —Economic/Communications Major, University of Pennsylvania

" College is the best place to approach new experiences since there are virtually no responsibilities compared to the 'real world.' Be sure to make that freedom worthwhile. "
   —**Physiology Major, University of Michigan**

" Don't expect to recognize yourself four years from now. "
   —**English Major, Vassar College**

Congratulations! I hope that you have enjoyed *College Unzipped: An All-Access, Backstage Pass into College Life, from All-Nighters and Exam Nail Biters, to Tuition Fees and Getting Your Degree.* All that's left to say is: Enjoy and good luck!